PETER SWAN

SETTING THE RECORD STRAIGHT

PETER SWAN

SETTING THE RECORD STRAIGHT

PETER SWAN

WITH NICK JOHNSON

I would like to dedicate this book to my wife and family who have provided their love and support during good times and bad. Also to the memory of Gary Swan.

First published 2006

STADIA is an imprint of
Tempus Publishing Limited
The Mill, Brimscombe Port,
Stroud, Gloucestershire, GL5 2QG
www.tempus-publishing.com

British Library Cataloguing in Publication Data.
A catalogue record for this book is available from the British Library.

ISBN 0 7524 4022 5

Typesetting and origination by Tempus Publishing Limited.
Printed in Great Britain.

Contents

Foreword

PETER SWAN — BY FAR AND AWAY
A WONDERFUL CENTRE HALF

Nineteen caps was meagre reward for such a talent as Peter
Swan possessed. Without taking anything away from the
glorious England team that won the World Cup in 1966, it
is my considered opinion that the team Walter Winterbottom
created prior to the 1962 World Cup was better.

I am firmly of the mind that, should injury not have
deprived us of three key players prior to the 1962 World Cup
in Chile, England would have progressed to the final and
possibly won it. The loss of Bobby Robson, Bobby Smith
and Peter Swan ripped the heart out of Winterbottom's
team in Chile and, with all due respect to the two Bobbys,
the loss of Peter Swan was felt the greatest.

We all make mistakes in life. Mistakes are what we men
call experience and should Peter not have made a mistake
when young, one that ended the career of an outstanding
centre half, his experience and skill as a top-class defender
would have ensured he would have been a part of England's
successful team of 1966. Of that I am sure. It is not for me to

pass judgment on anybody, particularly for mistakes made when young. In this book, Peter gives his personal account of matters; better he does that than anyone else.

What I can comment upon is Peter as a man and a footballer. Peter and I have been pals for over forty years and I feel fortunate to count him among my close friends. When he invited me to pen a foreword to his book, I had no hesitation in accepting. Peter was a breathtaking player; one who, in the days before football was subjected to hyperbole, was termed 'an outstanding pivot'. His perfect physique made him a handful for opponents and, for a big man and a centre half, he possessed outstanding ball control, passing, tackling and heading ability. This football package was wrapped up in the most genial of personalities, albeit one that was too trusting of people at times.

Peter also possessed a fine footballing brain which seemed to enable him to read the minds of opposing forwards. Graft on his awesome physique and you had a defence in itself. In those heady days of the early sixties when Tottenham Hotspur became the first club to win the League and cup 'double' in the twentieth century and did so with such great style (and this on Christmas pudding pitches), the only club really to challenge their dominance was Sheffield Wednesday. Without doubt one of the finest of all Wednesday players at that time was Peter who, no matter how tough the going became, remained unmoved like some rock in a raging sea.

I, for one, am glad Peter has decided to commit his story to book form. It is high time he offered his account of things, related the events and story of an international-class centre-back whose career was terminated far too early and who has had to live with the repercussions of having committed one mistake in his salad days.

Enjoy this book and his story, it is the story of a great centre half and a wonderful human being. Some cynics might be given to say 'but not the story of a great man', but as you will hopefully realise from Peter's story, there are no great men, only men.

Jimmy Greaves
2006

Acknowledgements

I would like to thank first of all my co-author Nick Johnson for helping me to write this book. It has been a lengthy, but rewarding process.

Thanks to Holly Bennion and Rob Sharman at Tempus Publishing for their efforts.

I am also grateful to my old mate Jimmy Greaves for writing the foreword.

For sharing their memories and helping to fill in the gaps, I'd like to thank the following people (listed alphabetically): Joe Ashton, Keith Brown, Peter Cooper, John Forrest, David Layne, Gordon Sorfleet and Derek Spence.

Others who have helped in various ways during the writing of this book include: Jonny Dennis, Helen Johnson, Colin and Paula Sedgwick, Peter Swan jnr, Peter Thompstone, Wayne Vaughan and Tom Wright. Thanks also to the staff in the Local Studies Department at Sheffield Central Library.

Introduction

My first ever conversation with Peter Swan did not get off to a promising start.

After securing a commission to write a magazine feature on Peter in the mid-1990s, I made a phone call to his pub in the hope of arranging an interview. I introduced myself as a journalist and there was a brief pause before Peter replied, 'You guys have been chasing me for thirty years.' It was not a response I was prepared for, but I assured Peter that I wanted to write about his whole career, not just the so-called 'match-fixing' scandal. Sensing his continuing reluctance to be interviewed, I offered to meet him for an initial chat without any obligation. This met with Peter's agreement and I travelled to his pub the following week.

When I met Peter, I repeated my intention to cover his career in general and offered to let him see the feature before it was submitted for publication. To my relief, he readily agreed to the interview and we sat down in a quiet corner of the pub. I recall him joking that the locals referred to his hostelry as 'The Crooked Swan' – a self-deprecating aside which made me warm to him immediately. With the tape recorder switched on, Peter patiently answered my questions. When the interviewed was concluded, I reminded Peter that he would be shown the finished article before submission. 'No, it's okay, I'll trust you,' he said. By the time I got round to taking the published article to Peter, one of the pub regulars had already taken a copy of the magazine to him. He told me that he was pleased with the piece, saying, 'It's the first time anyone has written exactly what I've said.'

A decade after our first meeting, I was delighted when Peter asked me to work with him on his autobiography. I had no hesitation in accepting because I felt it was a story which needed to be told. From humble beginnings in a South Yorkshire mining village, Peter went on to star at the highest level in English club football and made 19 consecutive appearances for England. We will never know what he might have gone on to achieve had the scandal not halted his career when he was at his peak.

There have been inaccuracies told about the scandal over the years and Peter wanted to give his account of what happened, hence the title of this book: *Setting the Record Straight*.

Peter and I have spent many hours discussing his life and career. Faced with seemingly relentless questioning, he has spoken with refreshing candour, never once refusing to answer a query, even when forced to revisit periods in his life he would no doubt rather forget.

It has been an honour and a privilege to have been trusted with the task of putting Peter's thoughts and recollections down in print, telling the story of his remarkable life. I hope you enjoy the journey.

Nick Johnson
2006

1

'Are You Prepared
to go to Jail?'

'Are you prepared to go to jail?' The question posed by my solicitor, Mr Arnold, hit me like a ton of bricks.

'I'm not, no,' I replied, struggling to take in the enormity of what he was saying.

'Well, you could be going to jail,' he warned.

At that moment I realised for the first time that something big was going to happen.

How had it come to this? I was a footballer at the top of my profession, playing for Sheffield Wednesday and England, when *The People* newspaper ran a sensational story about a 'match-fixing' scandal involving myself, David Layne and Tony Kay. David and I were teammates at Sheffield Wednesday and Tony had also played for the club before moving to Everton.

The People claimed that the three of us had been bribed to fix the result of a game between Wednesday and Ipswich on 1 December 1962. The fact was that we had not fixed the game. We had each placed a bet on Ipswich to win, which they did, but none of us had done anything to affect the outcome of the match. However, a police investigation resulted in David Layne, Tony Kay and myself being charged with conspiracy to defraud bookmakers.

It had appeared at one stage that we were in the clear when a clerk from David Layne's solicitors called in to see David one day at the café he owned in Sheffield, saying he had some good news. 'I've come to tell you that it looks as if they're dropping the case against you lads,' he said. 'It's all done with, so that's it.'

With that in mind, David went on holiday to Cornwall, thinking that everything was going to be alright. It turned out, however, to be a false dawn. By the time David returned home from his holiday, someone had apparently put some pressure on to make an example of us and made the situation even worse, so we were in deep trouble.

The case was first heard at Mansfield Magistrates Court before being switched to Nottingham Assizes. Journalist Mike Gabbert, who wrote the story in *The People*, was called as a witness. I'd met him briefly when he came to my house and accused me of helping to fix the Ipswich game, which I denied because it wasn't true. But he stood up in court to testify and said I'd confessed to everything. I couldn't believe what I was hearing because it was totally untrue. I fixed a stare at Gabbert as he was giving evidence, desperate to catch his eye. But he wouldn't look at me. He refused even to glance in my direction.

Under cross-examination, Gabbert admitted he had 'left things out' from the answers I gave him. It also later emerged that Gabbert had lied under oath. He claimed he had collaborated with the police during the course of his investigations, but a police officer told the court that *The People* had stated they would only provide information once the story had been published.

It was so frustrating to have to sit there and listen to people accuse me of doing something I hadn't done. I was determined to set the record straight and didn't hesitate when I was offered the chance to stand in the witness box and face questioning. Mr Arnold tried to talk me out of it, pointing out that I did not have to go in the witness box.

But he failed to persuade me. 'I want to go,' I insisted. 'I want to have my say and explain that happened.' When I faced the prosecution lawyer, everything I said was turned round. He cut me to pieces, saying that similar incidents to the one we got involved with had been going on regularly. I could only answer 'yes' or 'no' to the questions he was asking me. I was stopped as soon as I started saying anything else. They're very cute these lawyers and I was tied in knots. There was absolutely nothing I could do about it.

Looking back, I wish I hadn't gone into the witness box. I should have taken the advice and stopped out, but I'm an awkward bugger and I thought I could have my say. But it didn't help at all. If anything, it probably made the situation worse.

Addressing the jury, Mr Peter Mason QC said:

Friday last week was a very sad day. You heard an esteemed international footballer give evidence that he had made a dishonest bet, that he had placed a bet on two football matches which he knew were fixed. You may think it took some courage for Peter Swan to go into the witness box and before this court in public give that admission.

Mr Mason said that the jury might think that I had committed a flagrant breach of one of the most important rules in the Football Association rule book. He went on:

You may wonder in view of that how much is left of the playing career of Peter Swan. Of course, certain other proceedings may follow these, certain other enquiries may have to be made by the Football Association and you may think that the probability is that this man's professional career is in ruins about his feet whatever may be the result of this case.

I say these things because they are important in this manner: that Peter Swan from the very first moment he acted as he admitted he did, from the moment he placed that bet on these football games, had a guilty conscience. He was a man who knew right from the start that he had done wrong, he was a man who knew what the peril was if the matter came to light. He doesn't ask for sympathy, he asks only that you discharge your oaths and hear this case according to the evidence.

Mr Mason reminded the jury of the charge against me and said I was not accused of placing dishonest bets but of being party to an agreement to ensure my team lost and it was to that that the jury had to direct their minds. He added:

You will, of course, pay regard to the fact that he has never been in any sort of trouble before and that goes into the balance in his favour. The balance has got to go down firmly on the side of the prosecution before you can convict.

Association football is a rough game and there are some rough people playing, but that's no reason for doing rough justice. Justice is a delicate and very nice thing and you have got to be sure that it is done in this case. Peter Swan has been guilty of telling lies to the police. He has been guilty, if that be the right word, of admitting his discreditable conduct to newspaper reporters. But do these matters mean that he has been guilty of this criminal offence?

Has it been proved, have the prosecution established in the way in which they have to establish before guilt can be brought home, that there was this agreement to ensure that the match was lost? Unless you can be sure, unless you can say there is no reasonable doubt about it, having heard the evidence, can you convict him? I submit to you the evidence has far from proved this charge on this indictment and that Swan is entitled at your hands to be acquitted.

Summing up, the judge, Mr Justice Lawton said, '*The People* newspaper didn't try them. They made allegations. We do not have trial by newspapers, we have trial by jury and it matters not what *The People* said about these two men. What matters is your verdict.' The judge added that the police had investigated thoroughly and they couldn't find another bet that we'd placed on any other game.

Apart from the mauling I had received in the witness box, everything had appeared to be going well. I'd received some great support from Mr Arnold who was a brilliant fella. It was a very worrying time of course, but he helped me a great deal. He was always positive and happy. He believed everything I said and he'd keep my spirits up by saying, 'You're okay, there are no problems.'

Mr Arnold's attitude made me feel confident about the outcome and I was certainly not prepared for the bomb-shell that was about to be delivered when the day of the verdict arrived. Mr Arnold collected me in his car, just as he had done every morning while the court case was going on. We were sat together in the car and about to set off on our journey when, right out of the blue, he gave me the warning about going to jail. It was as though he knew what the outcome would be. These solicitors must get to know by talking to their colleagues.

On 26 January 1965, just over two years after the Ipswich match, I was faced with the prospect of losing my livelihood and going to prison. David Layne was tried separately after pleading guilty. He had been advised by his barrister that if he pleaded not guilty, all the evidence against him, which included affidavits saying that it was a one-off incident, would come out and incriminate myself and Tony Kay.

He was told that if he pleaded guilty, none of his evidence would come out and be used against either of us.

David then went out for lunch and considered his options. When he returned and appeared in court, he pleaded guilty and was taken to Lincoln Prison along with another footballer, Ken Thomson. That was on the Friday and David was remanded in custody over the weekend before returning to court for sentencing the following Tuesday.

The jury retired to consider their verdict and spent just under an hour deliberating before returning to court. I waited with Tony Kay for the decision. The trial had lasted eleven days and there was a sense of relief that it was coming to a conclusion. But at the same time, my solicitor's words were ringing in my ears, telling me to that I had to be prepared to go to prison. The tension was mounting as a deathly silence fell over the court. I steeled myself, clenching my fist, as the foreman of the jury prepared to deliver the verdict.

I can still hear the judge saying we had been found guilty of conspiracy to defraud. We were both sentenced to four months in jail and fined £100. My whole world came crashing down and I'm not ashamed to admit that I just broke down and cried. I get emotional thinking about that moment even now. I'd got a wife and four young kids and I was going to jail, leaving them at home. What would happen to them? I felt helpless.

There was not even a chance to say goodbye to anyone before we were bundled off. The police put handcuffs on us, marched us out and sat us on the bus. It was then that the realisation set in that I was going to prison. I was with the other convicted people from court and we were taken to Lincoln Prison.

At the end of the trial, a total of ten players were found guilty of conspiring to defraud bookmakers. Jimmy Gauld, who was the ringleader, was handed a four-year prison sentence and ordered to pay £5,000 costs. The other players convicted were: Brian Phillips (Mansfield), Jack Fountain (York), Dick Beattie (Peterborough), Sammy Chapman (Mansfield), Ron Howells (Portsmouth) and Ken Thomson (Hartlepool). I'm told there were others who were involved in match-fixing who escaped punishment, including one high-profile figure who went on to enjoy a lengthy career in management. *The People* were due to expose him the week after but they were prevented from printing any further revelations.

Gauld had a network of lower league players who rigged matches. The match-fixing that was going on at that time only came to light after Bristol Rovers' goalkeeper Esmond Million conceded two soft goals in a game against Bradford Park Avenue in April 1963. After being confronted by his manager, Bert Tann, he confessed to letting the goals in. During the resulting case at Doncaster Magistrates Court, Gauld's name was mentioned. Gauld wasn't charged, but *The People* approached him and he admitted everything. He agreed to co-operate with their investigation into match-fixing in return for a payment of £7,240. Gauld knew David Layne from their time together at Swindon and he must have passed his name on, even though David had not been involved in match-fixing. His only crime had been to bet on a match he was involved in.

It was stated in court that Gauld made £3,275 out of bets from 1 April 1960 to 20 April 1963. The judge told him:

> Over a long period and from one end of this kingdom to another, you have befouled football and corrupted your friends and acquaintances. You are responsible for the ruin of footballers of the distinction of Kay and Swan and you have ruined the life of an intelligent man like Thomson. I have not forgotten the tens of thousands of ordinary citizens who find relaxation in watching professional football. For their shillings they got not a match, they got a dishonest charade.

Going to prison was a very demeaning experience. How a criminal could want to keep going back to jail, I'll never know. The experience should be enough to put anyone off for life. When I first got there, my clothes were taken from me and I was left to stand there completely naked while they examined me. They look to see if you're clean and check that you haven't smuggled anything in.

After the examination, I was given a prison uniform and then shoved in a cell with other prisoners. Just using the 'toilet facilities' in the cell was degrading. There were two others in my cell and I was handed a little pot to use which stayed there until the next morning. I would be sat on the pot with two fellas just a few feet away. The routine each morning was to 'slop out', which meant carrying the pot to the toilet block, washing it out and then returning to the cell.

They'd take you out of the cell to walk around the prison yard, under supervision, for half an hour and then put you straight back. Then it was back to doing nothing, just sitting in the cell until meal time. The meals, which were basic, were shoved under the bars. When you don't know anything about that way of life, it's very hard to adapt.

It was a position that I never imagined in my wildest dreams I would find myself in, but all of a sudden, I was there. I didn't consider myself a criminal, so it was an especially shocking experience. I got very depressed and there were many times when I just curled up on my bunk bed and started crying.

Things improved when I was moved, along with David and Tony, to a prison at Thorp Arch, near Leeds. Being at Thorp Arch was like being in the army because it's an open prison where you're given jobs to do. We were working on making camouflage nets at first and then they put us on the gardens.

The governor called us to his office before we were locked up and said, 'Keep out of the way and don't listen to any criminal. Do as you're told and the time will fly past for you. Keep your noses clean and don't do anything to make yourself stay here longer than you have to.' He then added, 'I don't think you should be in here.'

It turned out to be good advice because the other prisoners were always bragging what crimes they had committed. They were talking about ways to break into a house and things like that. With all the tips on offer, I could have come out of prison and turned to burglary if I'd wanted. But I always kept myself to myself and tried to keep quiet as much as possible.

We were also warned by the governor that prisoners sometimes conned their way into the houses of people they had been in prison with once they had been released. Apparently, it had been known for a criminal to tell the wife of someone who was locked up that they were going back to prison the following week and their husband wanted some money.

In one of my phone calls home, I told my wife Norma to be on her guard against any such possibility. I said, 'If anyone comes knocking at the door saying they've come from Thorp Arch or Lincoln Prison with a message from me, you should not let them in.'

There were no real problems at Thorp Arch. As well-known footballers, the other prisoners accepted us. There was the odd comment made, but nothing to talk about really. We played football a lot of the time. The governor arranged games for us and sometimes we'd play three times a week. In Lincoln Prison we had been treated just like normal prisoners, but the open prison was like being in the Army.

As well as David, Tony and myself, there was the old Portsmouth player Ron Howells, who'd also been at Scunthorpe and Walsall, along with Brian Phillips, who went to Mansfield after leaving Middlesbrough.

Jimmy Gauld was kept away from us, no doubt for his own safety. I think the authorities knew he would have been hammered if he'd been put with us. It's amazing how many prisoners came up to us and asked if we wanted them to sort out Gauld. They knew we were bitter about him and offered to 'get him' in return for payment. But it wasn't made clear exactly what they would have done to him if we had accepted the offer.

I was disappointed with the lack of help from our union, the Professional Footballers' Association. Before we were even found guilty, they refused to get involved because they said the case was 'too big' for them. When we were at Thorp Arch, the PFA chairman, Cliff Lloyd, came to see us and he asked me if my wife and family had enough money to survive. But at that time I was still annoyed with the way the PFA had abandoned us leading up to the court case, so I told Lloyd that I didn't want anything from them.

Sheffield Wednesday manager Alan Brown also let us down. Before we were sentenced, he promised to do anything he could to help David Layne and myself. But Cliff Lloyd told us during his visit that we could not expect any support from Brown. 'I saw Alan Brown at a dinner last night and he said he didn't have time for either of you,' said Lloyd.

Brown's reaction was disappointing, but Wednesday's general manager, Eric Taylor, didn't turn his back on us. He came to see us in prison and that was very much appreciated. It was typical of him because he was an honourable man who I had a lot of respect for.

I didn't want my wife Norma to see me in that environment, so I told her to stay away on visiting days. I didn't really want to see anybody, but of course Norma did visit and there were other family members and friends who also came. At visiting time, we were taken to a room where we would meet our visitors. It wasn't a pleasant experience, having to sit behind a table with someone at the other end of the table.

It was a very difficult time for my family but, from the moment the scandal broke, I was given tremendous support

by them and they tried to help in any way they could. When
the story came out, I gathered various members of my family
together one night and told them exactly what had happened,
explaining that the only thing I had done was to have a bet.
All the talk of me being involved in bribery, I added, was a
load of rubbish. They believed what I had to say and never
criticised me.

My seven brothers, who were all miners, got involved
in fights in my home village, sticking up for me. They'd be
in the local pub and someone, no doubt fuelled by booze,
would start saying things about me, referring to the case.
They would call me all sort of names and my brothers
wouldn't stand for it. The people who were shouting the
abuse weren't from the local village who knew me and my
family, they were outsiders stirring up a bit of trouble.

There is no doubt that it was a testing time for Norma
while I was in prison. As well as looking after four kids,
she had to put up with some nutters on the phone. There
were people who sympathised and wished me good luck,
but there were a lot of cranks making abusive calls and
we had to have the phone monitored by the police. I
also received threats in the post. I had of course let down
Wednesday supporters who were no doubt disappointed
about what had happened, but I don't think the threats
came from fans.

I have to say that the Sheffield people, particularly those
in Stannington where we lived, were brilliant. You got the
odd one here and there shouting things like, 'You bent bastard.' But on the whole, we had a lot of support from those
who lived near us. When I was in prison, our neighbours
really looked after Norma, rallying round to do whatever
they could to help and I'll never forget that.

After being handed a four-month sentence, myself,
Tony Kay and David Layne ended up serving ten weeks.
I couldn't wait to leave prison and when the release date

came everything was arranged in secret to avoid the waiting members of the press.

David was released three days before Tony and myself due to the fact that he had been on remand. Despite the fact that it was six o'clock in the morning, there were still plenty of press people waiting for him to come out of the main gate. To help him try and avoid them, David was let out of the rear exit to meet his father who had arranged to collect him. He was carrying his football boots, which was a real give-away as to his identity, and thought he had been rumbled when a passing photographer pulled over in his car. 'Excuse me,' the photographer called over, 'can you tell me what time they're releasing David Layne?'

'No,' David replied, 'I haven't got a clue, kid.'

After driving off, the photographer realised his error, stopped and tried to get a picture of David who had by now set off running. David hid from him before dashing down the road to get in his dad's waiting car.

When it came to the day when Tony and myself were released, we were also let out early. We should have been released at about ten or eleven o'clock in the morning, but the prison officials agreed to let us out at six. A friend of mine called Jim Grundy came to pick me up from prison and took me straight home.

I had an emotional reunion with my wife and children. I had not seen my kids at all during my time in prison because I didn't want them to see me there, so a few tears were shed when I was reunited with them.

I was naturally delighted to be back at home with my wife and family after two and a half months locked up in a cramped, grey prison cell. But, at the same time, I was faced with the realisation that my football career was in ruins at the age of twenty-eight, when I should have been at my peak.

One thing was for certain – life would never be the same again.

2

Football Daft from an Early Age

I was born in South Elmsall, a mining village near Pontefract, West Yorkshire, on 8 October 1936. I have no memories of living in South Elmsall because when I was at a young age we moved about twenty miles away. Our new home was in another pit village, Armthorpe, near Doncaster, which is approximately five miles from the town's famous racecourse.

My parents, Len and Alice, raised seven of us, all boys, in a three-bedroom semi. My brothers – Len, Stan, Bernard, Billy, Terry and Mick – and I were kept in check by our mother who was the gaffer of the house. She was a dominant figure who ruled my father. He'd work a twelve-hour shift every day, get his pay packet on a Friday and, without even opening it, hand it over to my mother. With a big family to look after, she had to make the money stretch a long way because of all the things she needed to buy.

We also had a half-brother, Jack, who was raised by my grandparents. My mother gave birth to him out of marriage, which was a big taboo in those days. She was at a young age and it was a terrible thing to happen. In fact, the shame forced Jack's father to commit suicide, throwing himself down a mine shaft. When I was young, I thought that Jack was our mother's brother and it was not until I had left school that I was told the truth.

I would imagine that my mother's pregnancy would have been hushed up at the time and she probably rarely went out of the house for fear of people seeing that she was expecting. Then after she gave birth, the child was brought up by her parents in order to protect her reputation. In those days, it wasn't unusual for one member of the family to be raised by a relation. With such big families, that sort of arrangement was fairly commonplace and I can remember no end of families doing that.

My parents were proud working-class people who instilled the right values in us. They wouldn't stand for bad behaviour or foul language. In fact, I can't ever remember hearing my mum and dad utter a swear word when we were kids. Life was far from easy with nine of us living in such a small house, but we managed. There were double beds in both bedrooms occupied by myself and my brothers and we all slept together. It helped in winter time because you were really warm when there were four in a bed. It was lucky that we had no sisters because that would have complicated the sleeping arrangements! With the toilet down at the bottom of the garden, a bucket with Dettol or Domestos in it was placed in the middle of the bedroom, in case you needed to go during the night.

My father worked at the pit top as a shunter on the railway side. He was on a very low wage and had to do a lot of overtime to make ends meet. He never did an ordinary eight-hour shift. It was at least a twelve-hour day for him, seven days a week. Sometimes he'd even be doing fourteen or fifteen hours, so we rarely saw him because he was always at work. In winter, we'd get up for school as the old fella was coming in and by the time we'd come back from school, he'd gone to work again.

There was a 'knocker-up' called Mr McGarry who'd wake up all the mine workers who were on day shifts. They had to get up at half past four in the morning, so Mr McGarry was employed to make sure they got up on time. He carried a long pole to help him carry out the task. First of all he'd rattle the letter box and shout through it. Then, if no lights went on, he'd knock on the bedroom window with his pole. You heard him every morning at half past four, without fail. My mum paid him something like a shilling a week and he had to knock everybody up in the village, so he'd earn a lot of shillings.

My brothers all went down the pit. Len, as the eldest, was the first to start working there and we all followed suit. It wasn't a case of thinking about what type of job you wanted to do and then weighing up your options. Being from a mining village, you were more or less expected to work at the colliery.

They were generally hard workers in those days, but the money was poor compared to what people earn today. My mother had to take on jobs, as well as doing her household chores, to make ends meet. In the summer, for example, she would work in the farmers' fields. Once she'd got us all packed off to school, a lorry would come along and collect her and other women in the area and take them to the farms where they would pick peas and potatoes.

We were self-sufficient to a large extent with a garden full of vegetables and livestock, which were raised for kill-ing. There was a small play area for us kids at the top of the garden, with chickens in the middle of the garden and pigs at the bottom. When a pig was killed for Christmas, a retired butcher from the village would come along, armed with a tool known as a pig hammer. He would strike the pig's skull with the hammer, stunning it before cutting its throat and hanging it up to let the blood drain out. The pig's blood would be used to make black pudding. My brothers would fight for the pig's trotters, but I couldn't stand them. The feet would be cut off, cleaned and washed before being boiled, with the meat then picked out.

We'd always get the bladder from the slaughterman, blowing it up to play football, although it was more like a big beach ball than a football. The fact that it wasn't a perfect round shape meant that it would bounce about all over the place and the unpredictable movement helped you learn how to control the ball. I'd also use the bladder to help improve my heading ability, spending time throwing it against the house wall and heading it back. The hen pen was only a few yards away from the back door and my dad would breed about twenty cockerels which would be killed and sold at Christmas. Instead of wringing their necks, which some people did, he always used a knife with a long, thin blade to kill them. He would hold the chicken between his legs and push the knife down the centre of the head, killing it instantly. It was quicker than wringing the neck. The bird would then be hung up to let the blood drain out.

My father wasn't a big drinker and the only time my parents went out was on a Saturday night when they'd visit a local working men's club. It was left to my mum to discipline us lads. My dad never hit us, but my mum would knock us all over the place! It must have been a really difficult job for her to keep us all in check and do everything that was required at home. All the washing was done by hand, of course, because there were no washing machines in those days. She'd use a washing board and other labour-intensive devices.

All the cooking was done on an open fire with an oven at the side. My mother would give jobs to me and my brothers, so we did chores like peel potatoes and bring the coal in. The coal was always tipped out on the road when it was delivered from the colliery and we would have to bucket it in to the coal house.

People take for granted having a bath or shower in a bathroom, but we didn't have that luxury when I was a young lad. I can remember at a very young age being bathed in 'the copper', as it was called, in front of the fire. The copper bath would be filled with water and heated using a little coal fire underneath. The bath would also be used to boil the clothes. Because there was no time to heat up the water first thing in the morning, we'd be given a cold strip wash which was harsh, especially in the winter. Things improved in later years when the colliery installed boilers and put in bathrooms.

I was football daft from an early age. Even though my school was only five minutes from home, I'd set off an hour before the start of the school day and play with a tennis ball with my mates, trying to kick it between the various gate-posts along the way. Every time we scored, we'd move along to the next gate posts and, by the time we'd finished all the gateposts, it would be around nine o'clock and time to go in to school. My school shoes never lasted long because of the wear they got from kicking a ball about.

When I was at infants school, there was a playing field for the junior team at the side of our classroom and all I used to do was watch them playing football. I was in trouble all the time with the teacher for looking out of the window. At playtime it was always football; kicking a tennis ball. Then at night, I'd be throwing a ball up and heading it against the house wall or playing in the street with other kids. There was nothing like there is now in the way of entertainment for us. I must have been eighteen years old before I saw a television.

You made our own entertainment in those days and if I wasn't playing football, I'd be out bird-nesting with my mates. We collected eggs from nests built by blackbirds, thrushes and pigeons. Blackbirds' and thrushes' nests had about five or six eggs in and we'd put a pin prick at either end of the egg and blow it. The white of the egg would come out first and then the yolk, which we ate. To earn pocket money, we'd go bush-beating on a large estate in the Cantley area of Doncaster. We'd flush out the game birds which would then be shot. We were paid five shillings and given a pheasant or a rabbit to take home for the pot.

I'd often spend my school dinner money on sweets at a local shop. Then at dinnertime, I'd sneak into the dining hall with my mates who'd also spent up and we'd act as though we'd paid. We were given our dinner and that went on for a long time, without us ever getting caught out, because there was plenty of food to go round.

I was only a young lad when the Second World War was being fought, but I still have vivid memories of what happened at that time. When the air raid sirens first went off, our mother would shove me and my brothers under the kitchen table. That went on until an air raid shelter was built in the gennel behind our house. There was one gennel to about four houses, allowing access at the rear. The gennels were converted into air raid shelters, complete with bunk beds. If the air raid sirens went off, our parents would get us out of bed and take us to the shelter. I can remember hearing a lot of crying and screaming when we were woken up and all the lights had to be turned off. There was someone in the village who was responsible for ensuring this happened. 'Lights out, lights out,' he would shout as he went down the street.

The German bomber planes targeted Sheffield, which was about twenty miles away from us, because they were trying to destroy the steelworks. The distinctive hum of the planes could be heard as they went overhead and it was exciting for us kids because we wanted to see them. But we were hurriedly taken to the air raid shelter from where we heard the thunderous sound of the bombs being dropped. I can remember looking over towards Sheffield after the bombing raids had ended and seeing the skyline engulfed in flames. There was also an air raid shelter built at school. It was a Nissen hut, which was completely grassed over, so it looked as though you were walking into a hill. I think we only ever used it in practice because the raids were made at night time. We also carried gas masks to school.

Food was in short supply while the war was on, so we had to use ration books. With eight lads in our family, we had more ration books than most. I used to take the sweet coupons to school and do a deal with a kid I knew who came from a well-off family. Using the coupons I had given him, he would buy the whole allocation of sweets allowed and then split them with me.

Mine workers were excused army duties, so my father did not receive a call-up to join the fighting forces. The same went for my brothers who were old enough to be called up because of the fact that they were all miners. If you were a certain age, your parents had to give their consent before you could join the armed forces. During the First World War, my mum's brother John was due to serve in the Army, but my grandparents refused to give him permission. The next day, he went to work in one of the Doncaster pits and was killed following a roof-fall at the coalface. It was a cruel twist of fate because if his parents had signed the relevant consent forms, he wouldn't have been down the pit.

With poor parents like ours struggling to clothe their kids while the war was on, the offer of help from wealthy families was appreciated. When a large consignment of clothing arrived at school, parents with large families were given first choice to pick out the items they wanted. My mum came home with some knickerbockers for me and I was made to wear them, despite my protests. They came down to my knees and were worn with long socks. My mates ragged me something rotten when I wore them, but I was forced to use them until they wore out.

We only occasionally ventured out of the Doncaster area. Holidays were taken at Deal in Kent, staying with my mum's sister during the school holidays. We would also be taken to Cleethorpes every summer on a day trip with the local working men's club.

I was a bit thick at school and I learned more away from school because I just wasn't interested in the lessons. All I thought about was football. At Armthorpe Secondary Modern School, I was warned by a teacher called Mr James that if I didn't buck my ideas up in school lessons, he'd have me dropped from the football team. It has to be said that a lot of footballers in my day were dunces because, like me, all they thought about was football. I would be told off by my parents because my school reports were shocking, but I don't think they were really concerned about my education because it was just assumed you would go to work in the colliery. If you were a really bright lad, you might take your education further, but otherwise it was expected that you would go down the pit. I didn't even pass my eleven plus, which I was glad about because that would have meant going to grammar school and at that time it was all rugby and they didn't have a football team.

My mother's brother, Jim Griffiths, played for West Bromwich Albion. But he was the only footballer in the family, as far as I'm aware. My father certainly never played. One of my brothers, Terry, spent a year at Sheffield Wednesday and then signed for Rotherham. He made a few reserve-team appearances for them and then went into non-League football with Selby Town. After packing in football, he went on the club circuit as a singer in a group. Another of my brothers, Mick, played in the same school side as Kevin Keegan, who was also brought up in Armthorpe. After becoming a well-known player, Keegan gave an interview in which he commented on his upbringing, saying he had been brought up in a 'peasant village'.

His description upset a lot of people who lived in the area. I remember going to visit my mother around that time and she was up in arms over Keegan's comments. 'Have you heard what Kevin Keegan has said about our village?' she said, shaking her head.

My mum was very into psychic matters and she often used to go and see a spiritualist. There was a picture in our sitting room she was very fond of, which had belonged to her mother. But my dad couldn't stand it because it felt as though the eyes in the picture followed you around the room. One particular day, after the picture went missing, she lined us all up in the kitchen and said, 'Who's seen your grandmother's picture? Who's moved it?' We all stood there shaking our heads and denying any knowledge of its whereabouts. 'I'll find out,' she said. 'I'll know where it is. Your grandmother will come back and tell me where it is.' The next morning, she went straight outside, looked under the chicken hut and found it. It turned out it was my dad who had put it there! After getting fed up of feeling the eyes in the picture following him every time he went into the room, he decided to try and get rid of it, but failed. The picture was hidden in an unlikely place and how Mum knew where to look for it, I'll never know.

As my interest in football continued to grow, I started to go and watch my local team, Doncaster Rovers. They had a good Second Division side then and were always challenging for promotion. Peter Doherty was the player-manager and they had some good players. Sid Bycroft, an ex-copper who played for Doncaster, was my hero. He was a great big centre half who'd head a ball and nothing got past him. Ken Hardwick was in goal and there was a centre half called Bill Patterson who they sold to Newcastle. He must have had an influence on me because, looking back, I think I was a bit like him as a player. At full-back there was a player called Brian Makepeace. Clarrie Jordan was another of my heroes and I ended up playing with him at Sheffield Wednesday. He was a nice man, a real down-to-earth type. I remember a player called Ralph Maddison getting a lot of stick from the crowd. As a young lad, I couldn't understand why they got on to him. He was a workhorse type of player and the fans didn't like him at all. He always gave his all and I couldn't understand why he faced such criticism. I used to come home and tell my dad, 'They've been on to Maddison again.'

If I wasn't watching football, I was playing it. I'd eat, sleep and dream about football and all I really thought about was the next game. Football was like a drug and I was well and truly hooked.

3

'I'm Going to Put You in the Middle of Defence'

I have a female teacher called Miss Griffiths to thank for turning me into a centre half. Who knows how things would have turned out if she hadn't switched me from the right wing.

Miss Griffiths ran the school football team in the juniors. I had fancied myself as a winger because I was pretty quick as a young 'un, but Miss Griffiths saw something in me that no one else had seen and when the team was short of a centre half, she played me there. 'You haven't got an intellectual's brain, but you've got a footballer's one, so I'm going to put you in the middle of defence,' she said. It proved to be an inspired move because I remained in the same position from that day on.

It was unusual for a woman at that time to be interested in football, but Miss Griffiths liked her sport and wasn't afraid to make her point if she saw something she didn't like. She used to have a go at me when I tried to play the ball out instead of just hacking it clear. 'Stop faffing about with it Swan, get the ball away,' she'd shout from the sidelines.

My mother would sometimes come and watch me play for the school team, but I always dreaded it when she did because if anyone shouted anything at me, she'd have a go at them. It's amazing how many arguments there were between parents during those school games.

A group of travellers who sold household goods and clothing were regular visitors to our house. They were of Romany origin and parked their caravans just outside the village. Because my mum was so superstitious, she was frightened of them. She thought the gypsies would put a spell on her if she turned them away, so no matter what they were selling, my mum would buy from them. She'd even buy things that she didn't need and my dad would play hell with her. When my mum told the gypsies about my footballing exploits, several of them would sometimes turn up and watch me play in the school games.

The footwear we used was basic, to say the least. My dad would knock strips of old leather – called 'bars' – into the soles of my boots to form studs. There would be two bars on the sole and one on the heel. I don't think I had any proper football boots until a pair were bought for me at Christmas when I was about fourteen.

I played in the secondary school team after moving up from the juniors, playing with and against lads who were two or three years older than me. I was twelve and the average age of the others was fifteen, but I didn't find it a problem playing against older lads. Alan Finney, who I later played with at Sheffield Wednesday, was in the side and he was three years older than me. I recall playing in a game against Hatfield School just after I'd moved up to the senior school. Straight from the kick-off, the centre forward played the ball to Alan who was playing inside forward and he went right through the opposing team, holding off a number of challenges before scoring. I'll always remember it because it was a brilliant goal.

A teacher called Les Horner, who was a former professional footballer, ran the first team in the senior school. He had played for West Brom and Walsall as a centre half. Mr Horner was a fully qualified coach who opened my mind a little about the game and helped me refine my technique. As a young lad, I tended to go bulldozing in, but he told me I could be a hard and classy player at the same time. He encouraged me to play the ball out rather than just hoofing it up the pitch.

I would go down to watch the Armthorpe Welfare side when I was a kid. In those days the colliery teams played to a good standard. There was an eight-foot-high fence around the ground and I would stand in the adjoining farmer's field, waiting for the ball to come over. When a stray shot or clearance resulted in the ball coming into the field, I would try and head it back, nearly knocking myself out in the process! The balls were really heavy in those days, especially when wet because they retained the water. The laces in the ball could also be a problem if they weren't put in properly. If they were twisted and you headed the ball where the laces were, it would leave a mark on your forehead. Games rarely got abandoned due to the weather, so you would play through the rain with the ball getting heavier and heavier. Sometimes it was so heavy you could hardly kick it.

Football boots had a big toe cap, but they were more or less going out as I was coming into the game. The new Adidas boots that came in did not have a toecap and they were much lighter. They also had screw-in studs instead of the ones that had to be knocked in with nails.

At the age of fourteen, I was called up to the Doncaster Boys' side. They had trials every year and I nearly missed out because the trials clashed with a family trip to Hornsea for a week, which my mum had arranged. I was desperate not to miss out on the trials and explained my predicament to her.

'The Doncaster Boys' trials are on the week we're away,' I said.

'Well, what do you want to do?' she asked.

I told her I wanted to attend the trials, so arrangements were made for me to stay at home and let a neighbour look after me. It proved to be worthwhile because I did well in the trials and won a place in the side.

We had some good players in the Doncaster Boys' side. There was Billy Mordue who went on to play for Doncaster Rovers. Dick Lindley went to Lincoln City and there was a lad called Tommy Asher, an England Schoolboy international, who went to Wolves but failed to make it as a professional.

David Pegg, who went on to play for Manchester United and died in the Munich air disaster, played for Doncaster Tech. I played against him for Armthorpe School and he was a brilliant player. He was a left-winger, but he was one of those players who could play anywhere. He was really tricky and could beat three or four players with ease.

Being a member of the Doncaster Boys' side gave you a good chance of being picked up by Doncaster Rovers and I dreamed of playing for them. But my hopes were dashed when my father read an article in the *Yorkshire Post* newspaper, quoting Rovers' manager Peter Doherty as saying he had signed all of the Doncaster Boys' team. Doherty or one of his trainers had taken me and the rest of the Doncaster Boys' side for a training session at the Doncaster Tech gymnasium and that's how the story got into the newspaper. My dad had come home from work and was sat there reading the paper before tea. Quizzing me, he said, 'What's this in the paper – have you signed for Doncaster?'

'No, I haven't,' I replied.

Reading Doherty's quotes out loud, my dad was clearly unhappy with what he had said. The old 'uns in those days were funny about things like that. 'Well, if he thinks that, we'll go to Sheffield Wednesday,' he said emphatically.

Martin Heavey was a scout for Sheffield Wednesday and he used to come to our house once a week for a cup of tea and a chat, building up a good relationship with my father. He was a great old man who worked at the pit, but the people in the village effectively froze him out and 'sent him to Coventry' after one incident. His 'crime' was to say that he'd never vote for Labour again because of something they had done. He'd always been a Labour man, like the rest of the people at the colliery, but he then said he was going to vote for the Conservative Party. After that, he was treated like an outcast and nobody in the pit would talk to him. Nothing changed my view, however, that Martin Heavey was a smashing fella who got quite a few players for Sheffield Wednesday, including Alan Finney who was also from our village.

Sheffield Wednesday were known as a yo-yo side at that time because they were up and down between the First and Second Divisions. I travelled with my father and Martin Heavey to meet Wednesday manager Eric Taylor and discuss my future. Taylor wore a collar and tie and looked like a man of authority. He shook my hand and asked me different things, like whether I'd be happy with the travelling and so on. He was also well spoken and, for a lad like me from a mining village, I thought he was very posh. But he wasn't at all unapproachable; he was a smashing fella. My father wouldn't allow me to sign for Wednesday at that stage, despite Heavey's best efforts as he praised my skills and pointed out that a career in professional football could be very lucrative. Sensing that a different approach was required, Taylor reached into his pocket and produced a duplicate of the cheque Wednesday had paid to sign Jackie Sewell from Notts County. Wednesday secured Sewell for a British record transfer fee of £34,500, which was a massive amount at that time. Taylor handed the duplicate cheque to my father and then turned to look straight at me. 'Maybe one day you might be worth this,' he said.

My dad's eyes lit up as he read the figures on the piece of paper he was clutching. That swung it and the relevant papers were swiftly signed. My dad was so chuffed that when he came home, he told everybody that he'd had a cheque for nearly £35,000 in his hand. It was actually against the rules for me to sign for Wednesday, because I was only fifteen and still at school. I should have left school at Christmas, but I stayed on until Easter because they wanted me to play for the school team in a competition. Wednesday got round the problem relating to my signature by getting me to sign an undated contract and then adding the date as soon as I left school.

It had been my dream ever since I was a young lad to become a professional footballer and after signing as an amateur for Wednesday, I was closer to achieving my ambition. But before I could turn my attention to football completely, I followed the path taken by my father and brothers and went down the pit straight after leaving school.

4

Sleeping on the Job

I played part-time as an amateur for Sheffield Wednesday while working at Armthorpe colliery. I actually thought Wednesday had forgotten about me at one point because it was well into the season and I hadn't heard anything from them. My dad said he'd write to Wednesday and ask if they'd got any complimentary tickets for a forthcoming game. After sending his request, he received a couple of tickets, along with a letter stating that I had to report to the ground on the following Saturday morning for a 'B' team game. It came as a relief to me to learn that I hadn't been forgotten after all.

As an amateur from the age of fifteen to seventeen, I travelled to train with Sheffield Wednesday every Tuesday and Thursday night after completing a tiring shift at the colliery. It was a bind travelling from Doncaster to Sheffield by bus twice a week. I had to take a bus from Armthorpe to Doncaster and then from Doncaster to the centre of Sheffield. Then I caught the tram from there to Hillsborough. And then of course I had to travel back the same way. I'm a bad traveller and I bet out of ten journeys I would have been sick about six times.

I worked in the pit as a lasher-on, which was a physically demanding job, keeping me busy for the whole shift. There was an overhead iron rope on pulley wheels which went down a tunnel called the main. The empty tubs went down the main and the full ones came back from the coalface. I lashed the empties on to go down to the coalface and took the full ones off for them to go to the pit bottom. The chains which were attached to the tubs were thick and heavy, so it was hard work. A big iron hook would be used to pull the empties. The full tubs came up an incline and as they went on to the straight, the chain slackened and you had to get them off quickly.

The unpleasant experience of working in the pit was made worse by the fact that I was always frightened of going in the cage which took you down to the coalface. It would be full with about eighteen men crammed in and sometimes it would jerk up and down, making you fear for your safety. There were accidents down the pit, of course. If you got an old chain which was very worn, for example, it would slide because it wouldn't grip on the rope. The tubs would go down the incline and create a pile-up, so anyone working there would be hit.

After working for a while as a lasher-on, I was offered another job in the pit as a pipe fitter. One of our next-door neighbours, Jim Boyer, was a gaffer in charge of that particular section and he gave me the chance to change jobs. Mr Boyer, who was a Sheffield Wednesday fan, called over to me one day as I passed his house. 'Young Swanny, you've signed for Sheffield Wednesday, haven't you? Can you get me any tickets?' After we chatted about Wednesday, he asked me whether I'd like to work for him as a pipe fitter. It sounded like an easier job than the one I already had, so I readily accepted the offer. Being a pipe fitter was like a plumbing job, connecting pipes to get the water running for the coal face.

Mr Boyer was keen to help me get as much rest as possible, so that I would be fresh and ready to play for Wednesday. I'd help to get all the material together for the job and then Mr Boyer would say to me, 'Right, I want you to do nothing. Get in that manhole there and get off to sleep. Get yourself fit for Saturday.' For safety reasons, there was a manhole every thirty yards or so, just in case anything happened and you needed to get out of the way. There was a seat in the manhole, which could be turned into a makeshift bed. Obeying Mr Boyer's instructions, I'd be asleep while they finished the job. When the job was finished, they'd give me a knock.

Sometimes I'd help them when the job needed to be done quickly, but otherwise I'd have a sleep. If I'd been caught, I'd have been sacked straight away. But there were about six of us working together and they were mainly from Jim Boyer's family, so there were no problems. There were phones in the manholes and if someone was coming round to make an inspection, I'd be woken by an urgent call from a workmate. 'The under manager is on his way,' would be the warning. Then I'd black my face with soot, to make it look as though I'd been hard at work, and get out sharpish! I must have slept most of the time during my three years at the pit.

A month after celebrating my seventeenth birthday, I signed as a part-time professional in November 1953. I earned around £3 a week in the colliery and £6 a week as a part-timer at Hillsborough, plus win bonuses. The twice-a-week training routine continued and I carried on travelling to the ground on the bus and tram. In fact, I played in the first team for quite a while before buying my first car, which was a Ford Anglia. After finishing work at the pit at two o'clock, I'd catch the bus from Doncaster about two hours later. I'd get to Sheffield at about five, arrive at the ground at six and train for a couple of hours before heading home.

It was a tough schedule because I'd be up at half past four in the morning when my dad would get us all up and we'd be down the pit for six o'clock.

With early starts during the week and football at the weekends, socialising was pretty much restricted to Saturday nights, which I usually spent dancing at the co-op in Doncaster. I used to go with Alan Finney and other lads from the village and I'd meet Doncaster Rovers players like Bill Patterson there.

As a young hopeful at Hillsborough, I was playing with the likes of Tony Kay, Johnny Fantham, Don Megson, Keith Ellis and Brian Ryalls, who all went on to make it with Wednesday. I mainly knocked about with Tony, but we all got on well.

Alan Brown and Johnny Logan were the trainers under Eric Taylor, so they would take the training sessions. Brown was a hard man who always used to be on to Tony Kay and myself in training, driving us to put more effort in. I learned a lot from Logan and he was a big influence on me as far as my defending was concerned. He'd come to me at half-time in a game and explain what he wanted me to do. 'Peter, you're doing okay and getting tackles in, but get them in harder,' he'd say. 'I want you to go through the player as well.' It was the first time someone had told me to go in harder. Johnny had been a hard player himself as a left-half for Barnsley and Wednesday. He was the type of trainer who didn't explain things very well, but he could show you what he wanted.

We weren't allowed on the pitch in training; we just used to do continuous laps of the pitch to build up stamina. We'd start by doing six to eight laps as a warm-up and then do middle and fast runs from the corner flag to the centre of the pitch. Then we'd walk and go to the back of the goals for a sprint, or do another combination of middle and fast until your legs were aching. It was a hard slog and together with another young player called Arthur Eukin, who failed to make it at Wednesday, I would sometimes avoid doing a few laps. The old wooden North Stand at Hillsborough, which was replaced many years ago, provided us with a good hiding place when we wanted a breather. We would do a few laps and then hide in the shadow of the stand before joining in on the sixth lap. The trainer couldn't see us because he would be at the other side and it wasn't obvious that we were missing because there would be so many part-timers running together.

The first team, reserves and youth team were all kept apart at that time, which was the old-fashioned way of thinking. When you were young, you didn't know whether you should even talk to a first-team player because it was very much an 'us and them' situation. You respected the older players, so they ruled the roost. Until you got more experience under your belt, they told you what to do. Some older reserve-team players would train with us part-timers. Occasionally, if you put on a spurt, the older players would have a go at you because they wanted to go at their pace and didn't want to let the trainers see that you were faster than them.

After signing as a full-time professional, I was naturally keen to impress in training, showing the trainers just how fit I was. But my enthusiasm saw me incur the wrath of Norman Curtis, who was one of the senior players. Curtis had looked after himself and was a fit man, but I was twelve years younger than him and naturally had the edge in terms of energy. Curtis was grouped with some of the other older players when we were running one day. As I was about to overtake the group, Curtis put his arm out to stop me from going past. 'Get to the back lad: you don't pass us,' he growled. He was a tough old player, so I obeyed his instruction and fell in line, not daring to try and forge in front.

The training was pretty much restricted to running at that time. We were sometimes given a ball at the end of the training session and allowed to play five-a-side in a tiny gym underneath the stand, but apart from that, we didn't see a ball until the Saturday.

I was pleased with the progress I was making in football and knew I was edging ever closer to a first-team call-up. But I then received a call-up which had nothing to do with football and which took me away from home for the first time in my life. I was called up for National Service.

5

Army Life with 'Snake-hips'

At the age of eighteen, I began a two-year stint in the Army. I was in the Royal Signals and did a year at Catterick in North Yorkshire before making the short move to Gallowgate camp in Richmond.

I was a Physical Training Instructor (PTI) in the Army. It was a training regiment and my job was to help train the new recruits. I would split the group I was training into about four teams of ten and then set them various exercises to do. 'To your left, right, reach and press,' I called out as I patrolled the various groups. The class would last about forty-five minutes to an hour. It was a cushy number because I took two classes a day at the most, having the rest of the time free to do what I wanted.

My stint in the Army did not put my football career on hold as we were allowed to play in every game we wanted to play in, so I was off every weekend. After making my first-team debut for Sheffield Wednesday while in the Army, I was in and out of the side. When Don McEvoy got injured, I got called up as his replacement. Then when McEvoy came back, I dropped out. He then got injured again, so I won another recall and so it went on.

I hated every minute of being in the Army at the time. When I look back, however, I realise now that I had a brilliant time. I wanted to play football and that was pretty much all I did during my time in the Army. My big mate was Eddie Colman who had just got into the Manchester United side. He was the rat-catcher of the regiment. The billets were wooden, so we had a problem with rats and Eddie would put poison down to kill them. Once we'd done our jobs, Eddie and I kept ourselves occupied by jogging or kicking a ball about together and things like that. We were young, so we didn't need to do a lot of stamina work to keep ourselves fit for matches. On a Friday afternoon, we'd be away playing football until Monday morning.

I played for the Royal Signals' football team along with several other lads who went on to enjoy good careers in the game. I still have a teamsheet for an Inter-Corps match against the Royal Army Ordnance Corps at Chilwell Sports Ground on 14 March 1956. As well as Colman, our side included Graham Shaw, Billy Punton and John Hannigan. Shaw played across the city from me at Sheffield United and won five full England caps. Punton, who was an outside left, also had a spell with United towards the end of his playing days. He spent most of his career with Norwich after starting out at Newcastle. Hannigan played for Sunderland, Derby and Bradford Park Avenue after leaving his native Scotland. Jimmy Melia was another player I played alongside in the Army. He was a typical down-to-earth scouser and a very tricky inside forward. He later managed Brighton and took them to the 1983 FA Cup final.

Playing for the RAOC side were Duncan Edwards and Trevor Smith. Edwards was of course one of the 'Busby Babes' killed in the Munich air disaster and you can only wonder what he'd have gone on to achieve. He was a real strong lad with legs on him like tree trunks. Smith spent most of his career at Birmingham and won a couple of England caps.

As well as playing football for the Army, I also played cricket. I'd played cricket at school and for the village side as a fast bowler on occasions when I was younger. I enjoyed playing the game, but it was never anywhere near as important to me as football. And I was put off playing cricket after one particular game in the Army. I played up to a bouncer and the ball struck me in the face. It frightened me and put me off to such an extent that I didn't play much cricket after that. On one of the rare occasions when I did pick up a bat again some years later, I played in a charity game which featured a number of Yorkshire players. Former England fast bowler Freddie Trueman was among them and I remember him effing and blinding as we sat around having a drink after the game. His language was terrible and he didn't care who heard him.

I saw Eddie Colman every day during our time together in the Army and we were more or less inseparable. He was a very funny lad, a real character who made you laugh all the time. No matter what you said to him, he'd say, 'Sure, baby.' That saying went round the camp and later went round the football teams. Eddie, who came from Salford, was a typical Manchester lad. He was quiet but he liked to be noticed and was never miserable.

Eddie was a brilliant player who made over 100 appearances for Manchester United before being killed in the Munich air disaster. He didn't get many goals, but he did score in the first leg of United's fateful European Cup quarter-final against Red Star Belgrade. Eddie was nicknamed 'Snake-hips' at Old Trafford because he could move his body and send the crowd the same way; it was unbelievable what he could do. I might be biased because he was my best friend, but I think that Eddie would have had a name as big as Pelé if he hadn't been killed.

When I got married to Norma during my last month in the Army in 1957, Eddie was my best man. We had to get married because Norma went to the altar pregnant. We would have got married anyway at some point, but in those days of course it was very much frowned upon for an unmarried woman to give birth. The wedding was in Sheffield at Shiregreen church. We'd been together about three years after meeting in Newquay when she was play- ing cricket with her dad. Her dad was bowling and she was batting when I was walking down the beach. I went behind the stumps, pretending to be a wicketkeeper, but really I was chatting her up! Then I saw her that night and we've been together ever since. She is from Sheffield and a mad Wednesdayite. Her dad took her to Hillsborough as a youngster and she would get passed down to the front of the Kop.

If things had worked out differently, I could have ended up playing with Eddie Colman at Manchester United. There were rumours when I came out of the Army that United boss Matt Busby was keen to take me to Old Trafford. Then a Wednesday player called Don Gibson, who was married to Busby's daughter, indicated the rumours were true. After one particular night game, just after I'd com- pleted my National Service, Don had a word with me. 'Do you fancy Old Trafford?' he asked.

'What do you mean?' I replied.

'Well, do you fancy playing at Old Trafford?'

'I don't know, really, I've only just got into the side here.'

Don drew closer and said, 'Between you and me, Busby's coming to see Eric Taylor about you.'

I believed what Don said and I'd have loved to have gone there because Manchester United have always been a top side. But I never heard anything else about it, so I can only assume that Taylor rejected Busby's approach.

Later on in my career, when I was with the England Under-23 squad, I was 'tapped up' by Ron Greenwood. Ron, who was in charge of the Under-23s, told me I could earn about £100 a week at West Ham.

One day, out of the blue, he asked me, 'Would you like to live in London, Peter?'

'Not really, but if the money is there you have to go for it because you only have a short career,' I replied.

Again, I never heard anything more, so I don't know whether West Ham did attempt to sign me. Any interest from clubs was kept from you. The manager wouldn't come to you and say, 'So and so wants you, but you're not going.' It was not like today, where players have the power and can pretty much change clubs at will. In those days, clubs held the upper hand and decided whether you stayed or not. Even when your contract was up, you more or less had to sign another one.

I kept in regular contact with Eddie Colman when we left the Army before his life was cruelly ended at the tender age of twenty-one. I'd gone home to Doncaster to visit my mother and father when it was announced on the radio that the plane carrying the Manchester United players home from their European Cup quarter-final against Red Star Belgrade, via Munich, had crashed. The details were sketchy and they didn't say how many people had been killed. After anxiously awaiting further news, I was devastated when it was announced that Eddie was among the dead. At the age of twenty-one years and three months, he was the youngest casualty of the crash. At first, I couldn't quite take in the fact that he had died. 'I spoke to him only the other day and now he's not here,' I thought to myself. I never met Eddie's parents, which is something I regret. I decided not to go to his funeral because I thought it would be too busy, packed with mourners, so I sent a wreath instead.

Having been a target for Matt Busby, it is sobering to think that I could have been on the plane along with Eddie and the rest of the 'Busby Babes' who perished in Munich, if things had turned out differently.

6

'Mr Taylor, I Think I'm Ready'

My elevation to the Sheffield Wednesday first team came after I received an invitation from manager Eric Taylor more or less to name myself in the side. Taylor came up to me one day before training and surprised me with his suggestion. 'Peter, when you think you're ready, come and knock on that door and tell me,' he said.

I thought to myself, 'Well, I could go and tell him that now.'

I went home and told my wife Norma what Taylor had said to me. 'I'm going to go in tomorrow and tell him,' I said.

After training and having a shower, I went straight to the manager's office, knocked on the door, put my head round it and saw Eric Taylor sat behind his desk. 'Mr Taylor, I think I'm ready,' I said.

He didn't question me and agreed to put me in the first team at the first opportunity. True to his word, Taylor handed me my debut at Barnsley in November 1955 as a replacement for Don McEvoy who was injured. I was nervous before the game, which is only natural, but as soon as I got out there the nerves went. I was up against Tommy Taylor, who later joined Manchester United and was killed at Munich. He was a good player, but I didn't find him as robust as people said he was. He wasn't a hard player, unlike most of the centre forwards in those days. It was a successful debut because we kept a clean sheet and won 3-0 with two goals from Roy Shiner and another from Albert Broadbent. The win took us up to third in the Second Division. Journalist 'Taffy' Williams, writing in the *Sheffield Star,* said:

> Eighteen-year-old Peter Swan, playing in his first game, had every reason for being satisfied with his display at centre half-back, for he showed a sound positioning sense, and was good with his head.

I made my home debut a week later against Middlesbrough. I was up against a centre forward called Charlie Wayman who'd been at Newcastle. Albert Broadbent missed a second-half penalty for Wednesday, which saved the club £50 because they had agreed to pay that figure to his former club Notts County for every goal he scored. I was on the winning side again as we beat Boro 3-1.

Another game early in my career was at home to South Yorkshire neighbours Rotherham. We suffered a 2-0 defeat, but 'Taffy' Williams acknowledged in his match report in the *Sheffield Star* that I had kept Rotherham centre forward Terry Farmer quiet. He wrote, 'Farmer did not do anything of note against Swan.'

I settled down quite easily because I'd got bags of confidence and I desperately wanted to be a good player. A Wednesday player called Jack Shaw used to say to me, 'Don't be big-headed. Be very cocky, but don't be big-headed about it. It's amazing what a difference it makes. When you're cocky on a field, you're confident.'

Jack was right because I used to strut about the field as if I owned the place and it did help. One of the things I did to project an air of confidence was to wear short shorts, which became my trademark. I came to wear short shorts following a conversation with one of my Wednesday teammates, Albert Quixall. He wore his big, baggy shorts rolled up. When I became a full-time professional, I asked Albert why he wore them like that and all he said was, 'An athlete doesn't wear baggy trousers, does he?' So after that I started rolling my shorts up, the same as Albert. I had some legs to go with it, so they thought I was a bit of a show off. I'd get some right stick at away grounds. People used to have a go at me over the way I wore my shorts, shouting out comments like, 'Hey, you big-headed twat.' But things like that never used to bother me.

There were other players at that time who wore them short, but I don't think there were any who wore them quite as short as I did. I wore them really short and it's a good job I had a jockstrap on! I started buying my own shorts, specially made by a Sheffield sports shop called Jack Archer's, which were smaller than the ones issued by the club. I had about two pairs made every season. They weren't baggy, just a nice fit. Nobody at the club knew that I had them made because I didn't tell anybody.

Jack Archer, whose shop was opposite the Sheffield United ground on Bramall Lane, also supplied us with football boots. Whenever you needed a new pair of boots, you had to go to Jack who would kit you out and send the bill to the club.

Soon after I got into the side, I had a run-in with one of the older Wednesday players, Don Gibson. When the teamsheet was pinned up on the noticeboard the day before a game, players would go up to it and look to see who was playing and who had been dropped. On this particular occasion, Gibson took a look at the teamsheet and then came straight over to me with a face like thunder. 'I've been fucking dropped because of you,' he raged.

'Why?' I replied, puzzled at the accusation.

'Because I'm calling for too many short balls off you.'

It was true that I was playing short balls to Gibson after winning possession, but only because he was calling for them! Eric Taylor wanted me to hit the ball upfield at the earliest opportunity as he believed there was a greater chance of scoring that way. Even though Gibson knew that, he was constantly looking for short passes. He blamed me for the fact that he had lost his place and played hell with me. In fact, I thought he was going to punch me. I was only a young lad, so I didn't know what to say to him.

We had a player called Walter Bingley who was wild and would kick his own granny. In one game our goalkeeper, Les Williams, went down to save the ball by a goalpost. The ball squirmed from his grasp and Walt lashed at it but missed and kicked Les right in the chest. Walt didn't bat an eyelid and just carried on with the game! Another example of Walt's uncompromising style came when he was warned by trainer Jack Marshall about the threat posed by a pacy winger he was due to face. With a shrug of his shoulders Walt said, 'Don't worry about him Jack, he can't run without legs!'

After a brief taste of first-team football, making four appearances over November and December, I was left out of the side for the rest of the campaign. It was a good season for Wednesday because they went on to win the Second Division title.

After missing the opening six games of the 1956/57 season, I made my first appearance in the First Division against Cardiff at Hillsborough. I received a call-up as a replacement for Don McEvoy who had suffered a knee injury. That put me up against my hero, Cardiff's Wales international centre forward Trevor Ford. In my schooldays, he was one of the top players and I'd pretend to be him when I was playing up front as a kid. But my excitement at playing against Ford ended abruptly when he hit me! I went into a tackle with him and as we were both getting up, he threw a punch which caught me on the chin. I thought to myself, 'He's my hero and he's chinned me!' That just made me more determined though and I roughed him up. Every time we challenged for the ball, I gave him some real stick.

Writing in the *Sheffield Star*, Fred Walters commented:

> Credit must be given to young Swan at centre half. It is no easy thing to have to face a player like Ford, for while Ford may not be the dangerous centre he was some while back, he is still one to be reckoned with.

My four-match run in the side came to an end following a 4–2 defeat at home to Arsenal. We had also conceded four goals at Manchester United the week before.

After a seven-month spell on the sidelines, I returned to the side for a game at Aston Villa in April 1957. I only played because of the late withdrawal of Ralph O'Donnell who had gone down with flu and it turned out to be a game to forget after I was played out of position as a full-back. I can remember thinking to myself that it would have been better to play a more experienced player at full-back and use me at centre half. That thinking proved to be right because I was out of my depth and didn't know which way to look as we lost 5–0. I never played at full-back again.

Taffy Williams summed up our performance in the *Sheffield Star*, describing it as 'very disappointing, lifeless and ineffective'. He added, 'Free from fear of relegation it was to be expected they would serve up some good football, but they gave a very poor exhibition against the cup finalists, so poor that they made Villa look a great side.' Commenting on my contribution, Williams said, 'Neither he nor Tommy McAnearney succeeded in their efforts to get a grip on the Villa inside forwards.'

Fortunately, my below-par display at Villa Park did not cause any lasting damage because after leaving the Army, I signed a full-time contract in time for the start of the 1957/58 season. Keith Ellis, Gerry Young and Alan Finney also signed contracts after completing their National Service.

As a full-time professional, I used to travel to Hillsborough with Norman Curtis and Billy Griffin, who also lived in the Doncaster area. I remember when I was travelling back to Doncaster with Norman and Billy one day; Norman was driving and Billy was in the front passenger seat while I was sat in the back. During journeys home, we'd often stick our heads out of the window and shout things to people. It would be nothing rude or cruel, we'd just be having a laugh. On this occasion, when Billy wound his window down and put his head out to shout to some people we were passing, Norman quickly wound the window up and trapped Billy's head. Norman wouldn't free him, so I think Billy travelled from Rotherham to Doncaster with his head hanging out of the window, pleading to be released!

Billy was a smashing lad and a good goalscorer who had the knack of being in the right place at the right time. He was a very frail lad, so he was put on a special diet to try and build him up. Billy would drink milk after training and he was told to eat a lot of potatoes. He boasted a good strike rate, scoring 20 goals in 35 appearances, but he failed to hold down a regular place and was transferred to Bury.

We experienced a difficult time at Hillsborough as a flu epidemic swept right through the club. Just about every player went down with it and the worst affected was Norman Curtis. He nearly contracted pneumonia, which would have been life-threatening in those days.

One of the leading players for Wednesday at that time was a centre forward called Roy Shiner. He was able to imitate a referee's whistle and it was a trick he used to good effect. Sometimes, when Roy was chasing a ball played over the top, he'd whistle and the defender who was in pursuit would pull up. That would enable Roy to gain a good few yards until the defender realised what had happened and it was often too late by then.

Another character at the club was Jack Shaw who used to have two pints of beer before he played. He'd always call in to a pub on the way to the game and have a drink. Imagine that happening now!

Manchester United were drawn to face Wednesday in the FA Cup at Old Trafford in their first game after the Munich air disaster. The game proved to be the turning point for me because Eric Taylor handed me a recall in place of Don McEvoy and from then on I was a first-team regular. Taylor was a brilliant man who'd worked up from being an office boy to being team manager and general manager. He was a smart man who was never out of a collar and tie and looked like a businessman. He was very shrewd and everybody respected him. But I can't remember him ever giving a bollocking to anybody and he didn't look like the type who could do that.

United's assistant manager, Jimmy Murphy, who was in charge of the team while Matt Busby battled for his life, scrambled a team together. Mark Pearson, who was a Sheffield lad, made his debut for United. I played with him later when he signed for Wednesday and he was a good player, but he wasn't consistent enough.

It was a highly emotional occasion with people crying – men and women. There were people gathered together in floods of tears. I felt emotional of course because of my close friendship with Eddie Colman. The ground was packed solid and there were many people outside as well. Every time one of the United players got the ball, the crowd seemed to gee them up and it felt as though we just couldn't win the game. In fact, I don't think any team would have won there that day. It was a game we just wanted to get out of the way.

One of United's debutants, Shay Brennan, scored direct from a corner. Alec Dawson completed the scoring after meeting a cross from Pearson in a 3-0 win for the home side. Dawson was a fairly straight up and down type of centre forward who didn't really give me too many problems. Playing at Old Trafford in front of nearly 60,000 fans was a massive stage, but I felt good and felt at home.

Eric Taylor was probably resigned to suffering relegation when he decided to put a few of us young lads in the side towards the end of the season. I kept my place after the Manchester United game while Tony Kay and John Fantham also began to emerge.

Ron Springett was signed from QPR and he took over from Brian Ryalls as the first-choice goalkeeper. It proved to be a very important signing as Springett was a key member of the side for a number of years. It was very rare that Ron dropped the ball and people used to ask him whether he had glue on his hands. He wanted to keep his family home in the south, so it was agreed that he would train in London during the week and travel up on the Friday.

Eric Taylor had been working in a combined role as manager and secretary. I can't remember Taylor ever giving us a team talk. All he would say before a game was to tell us to go out and enjoy it. He didn't know the game as far as tactics were concerned, but no one questioned that. Eric's idea was that as soon as I or any other of the defenders got the ball, we had to kick it upfield as far as we could and try and get it into the penalty area. Sometimes it paid off, but it wasn't pretty to watch.

Jack Marshall, who was a coach, advised players on different aspects of play. 'Jolly Jack' was his nickname because he was always happy. There were also a couple of trainers called Tom Walker and Sam Powell. They were the old type of trainer who were like father figures to us young lads. They'd sit down and talk to you, showing you things they wanted you to do. They would demonstrate rather than explain what they wanted because they weren't particularly good communicators. They were typical thick footballers who'd been kept on at the end of their playing careers and hadn't taken any coaching badges.

Wednesday had a reputation for being a yo-yo team at that time, flitting between the top two divisions. Going down to the Second Division made it a third relegation in just seven years and prompted the directors to make a radical change to the managerial set-up in the summer of 1958.

It was decided that Eric Taylor would remain as secretary and someone would be brought in to manage the team, so the post was advertised for the first time since the 1930s.

Harry Catterick was appointed as the new manager of Sheffield Wednesday just before the start of the season and he was to have a major influence on my career.

7

'Go Straight Through Him'

Harry Catterick arrived at Sheffield Wednesday after enjoying a good season at Rochdale and it was a big move for him. He was a hard man who took no prisoners and demanded respect. If you didn't do what he wanted, you knew you were in for it.

Catterick had not been Wednesday's first choice because, when the directors began their search for someone to take over the running of the team, Bill Nicholson was the first man they interviewed. He of course later led Spurs to the League and cup double.

We enjoyed a good start to the season, winning 4 out of our opening 5 games. Then we thrashed Sunderland 6-0 at home with Redfern Froggatt scoring a hat-trick. Sunderland had signed a big South African player called Don Kichenbrand. He looked like a big, mad bull and there was me, just a young player making my way in the game. But he was just like a kitten when it came to facing him. Albert Quixall got his name on the scoresheet in what proved to be his farewell Wednesday appearance before moving to Manchester United for £45,000, which was a British record transfer fee.

Quixall, with his blond hair, was dubbed 'The Golden Boy of British Football'. Matt Busby was rebuilding his team following the devastation of the Munich air disaster and Quixall was the first signing personally made by Busby after he recovered from the injuries he sustained in the crash.

Our first game after Quixall's departure was at home to Leyton Orient and it was Jim McAnearney who took the no. 8 shirt vacated by Albert. Redfern Froggatt scored both goals in a 2-0 win and I was pleased with my performance. Journalist David Nicholls recognised my potential, writing in his match report:

> I rate this gangling uncompromising centre half the most improved player around Hillsborough. He still has a long way to go. But the progress from the raw material of last season is so remarkable that he is obviously capable of becoming one of the most effective centre halves in the game. He is now beginning to use the ball, too.

We kept our winning run going with a 2-0 win at home to arch rivals Sheffield United, following goals from Redfern Froggatt and Roy Shiner. In the *Sheffield Star*, Ross Jenkinson compared me to one of my idols, United defender Joe Shaw, which was a huge honour. Jenkinson said, 'We have come to expect top-class displays from Joe Shaw almost as a matter of right. In this match, his opposite number, Peter Swan, produced something of the Shaw brand. His footwork was tidy, positioning correct, and recklessness curbed.'

Goals from Shiner, Fantham and Froggatt gave us a 3-1 win in the following game at Brighton. In his match report, journalist Peter Orr commented:

> Wednesday are sitting at the top of the Second Division and look sure to stay there judging by the display at Goldstone

Road. Wingers Wilkinson and Finney gave the Brighton defence a hectic time, but one of their strongest departments was the half-back line, in which Peter Swan was really outstanding.

Our 11-match unbeaten run was ended when we went down 3-2 against Liverpool at Anfield, giving Catterick his first defeat as manager. As well as the roar of the Anfield crowd urging the Liverpool players on, we also had to endure a shower of half-eaten meat pies which came from behind our goal in the second half! The referee had to call on the police to restore order. Despite the fact that we conceded three goals, we were praised for our defensive display. *Sheffield Star* journalist Ross Jenkinson observed, 'But for the brilliance and cool assurance of Wednesday defenders – Martin, Swan and Curtis in particular – the knock-out would have come before there was chance for reprieve.'

We continued to make good progress and opened up a three-point lead at the top of the table at Christmas. We were rewarded for our efforts with a bonus of £20 paid to every player! At that time we also had an unofficial win bonus paid by one of the directors, a gentleman called Mr Whitlam. He would pay us £10 for a win and £1 for every goal. It would be paid in cash straight after the match. If we were going to an away match, Mr Whitlam would get on the coach and use hand signals to indicate how much he was ready to pay as a bonus. Because we were winning regularly, we were raking it in. I was banking all my wages and living on the cash I received from Mr Whitlam.

One of the few setbacks we suffered that season was a 6-2 defeat at Fulham in March. We had an amateur called Mike Pinner who played in goal that day and he had an absolute nightmare. He was a posh lad who'd been signed from Corinthian Casuals. Mike was such a nice, polite lad, that he just about congratulated the opposition players for scoring! As the ball flashed past him and went into the net, he'd say something like, 'That was a good goal.'

Jimmy Hill, who of course later found fame as the host of *Match of the Day*, scored a hat-trick for Fulham. He was a tall lad, sporting the distinctive little beard he had for many years, who played as an inside forward. I can remember Tony Kay going into Hill with a hard tackle. It was fair, but Hill wasn't happy and he went right up to Kay and told him in no uncertain terms what he thought about the challenge. Kay responded by giving his beard a good yank and then running behind me, where he knew he'd be safe! Hill was a schoolteacher type who did well for the players in his role as chairman of the PFA, getting the maximum wage lifted. He wasn't anything special as a player, but he was gangly and awkward and could get goals.

A 1-0 win over Liverpool in midweek saw us promoted to the First Division. Skipper Redfern Froggatt got the crucial goal, firing home after meeting an Alan Finney cross. He had not scored since early January and had said he was saving his scoring for the promotion-winning match. Liverpool put us under plenty of pressure but they just couldn't score.

I didn't get much sleep in the build-up to the following game, at Bill Shankly's Huddersfield, following the birth of our second son, Gary. He joined sixteen-month-old Carl in the Swan household. Gary's arrival didn't really affect my performance though because I had a good game in a 2-1 win. Referring to the new addition to my family at the post-match dinner, Wednesday chairman Dr Andrew Stephen proposed a toast. 'To the young player I signed-on in the early hours of this morning – a bouncing eight-pound thirteen-ouncer,' he said.

As we prepared for the final home game of the season, against Barnsley, Charlton beat Fulham virtually to hand us the title. We beat Barnsley 5-0 with Roy Shiner and Redfern Froggatt scoring two goals apiece. We were not handed the Second Division championship trophy, however, because it was still with the engravers. Barnsley chairman Joe Richards was also the Football League president at that time and it was rumoured before the game that he wouldn't hand over the trophy because it would be too embarrassing for him to do so after a game involving his club. But Richards dismissed the speculation as 'utter rubbish', insisting he would have done his duty as League president if the trophy had been available. The Wednesday fans celebrated on the pitch after the game. The players and management gathered in the directors' box to acknowledge them. 'We want Shiner,' the supporters chanted. Shiner, who originated from the Isle of Wight and had a southern accent, was pushed towards to the microphone which was positioned at the edge of the directors' box. With his face still caked in mud and after a couple of false starts, he finally delivered a short speech. 'You know how it is, you miss 'em and you get 'em,' he said. 'This is the second time I've led the attack in a promotion season. Both times it's been a real pleasure.'

The editorial in the match-day programme naturally made reference to our promotion success. It read:

All smiles again! The old club has won promotion for the fourth time in post-war football, and the sixth time in the club's history. In the handing out of bouquets there must be one to Mr Harry Catterick who, in his first season as team manager, has had the pleasure of controlling a promotion-winning side. He has had his problems but it must have been satisfying to see our schoolboy signings such as John Fantham, Peter Swan and Tony Kay make the grade and firmly establish themselves.

Having followed an up-and-down pattern in previous years, many people probably expected us to make an immediate return to the Second Division. But we were determined to establish ourselves in the top flight and our performance on the opening day of the 1959/60 season sent out a warning to other teams. We went to mighty Arsenal and came away with a 1-0 win following a goal from John Fantham.

I felt that I had a good game against David Herd and the respected national newspaper journalist Ken Jones paid me a glowing tribute in his report on the match: 'Swan turned in a performance that completely overshadowed Mel Charles, his record-priced opposite number, who was making his First Division debut.' Arsenal manager George Swindin was not so generous, because he was quoted as saying that he didn't think we were a good side. That could have been sour grapes, of course, after seeing us win.

We had a good side and we continued to pick up some good results, notably a 7-0 victory over leaders West Ham in November. Keith Ellis, who scored one of the goals, had an important role to play in that game. He was told by Harry Catterick to go into the goalkeeper, who was called Noel Dwyer, with his elbows. That meant that Dwyer was looking for Ellis when the crosses were coming over, which was obviously distracting. As a result, he kept dropping the ball when Ellis went into him and a few of the goals came that way. Ellis used to practise the tactic of going up to keepers with his elbows and it certainly paid off that day.

The West Ham result was followed by a 4-0 win at Chelsea with John Fantham scoring twice, just as he had done against the Hammers. A little Scotsman by the name of Bobby Craig also got his name on the scoresheet. He was a mouthy little so-and-so and I ended up fighting with him in training one day, but it was a one-sided fight given the height difference! We both had to go and see Eric Taylor following the bust-up, but there were no lasting problems between us, it was just one of those things that happens in training.

Johnny Quinn was introduced into the first team after making the step up from non-League football. He was originally an inside forward before being switched to centre forward. John had a good football brain and played like they do today.

Don Megson was another lad who graduated to the first team at that time. He went on to become a very good full-back and eventually replaced me as Wednesday captain. Don was one of the hardest tacklers around, but he hardly ever got booked. His son Gary also played for Wednesday and has of course managed various clubs including West Brom and Nottingham Forest. The other full-back was Peter Johnson, who had been signed from Rotherham in the summer. He was signed as a centre forward, but got switched to defence.

As well as doing well in the League, we also enjoyed a good FA Cup run. Wins over Middlesbrough and Peterborough set up a fifth-round tie with Manchester United at Old Trafford. There were over 66,000 fans there to see us win 1–0 following a penalty from Tom McAnearney. I was at the centre of a controversial incident immediately before the goal. United's former Wednesday star, Albert Quixall, beat Ron Springett with a shot, but I got back to clear off the line. That is not strictly true, however, because the ball was over the line. I bet it was a yard over, but I hooked it out quickly and the linesman failed to spot that it had crossed the line. My clearance went to John Fantham who raced clear into the area before being brought down by Maurice Setters for the decisive penalty. That's football for you; sometimes you get breaks like that.

We then faced arch-rivals Sheffield United at Bramall Lane in the quarter-finals. The ground was full again for that game with over 61,000 in attendance. Over 3,000 were seated in a temporary stand which was erected on the old cricket pitch they used to have at Bramall Lane. In those days they really packed them in because there weren't the safety considerations they have in place now.

United always had a reputation as a footballing side, but manager John Harris seemed to alter their style that day and they played into our hands. They were just knocking long balls forward to 'Doc' Pace and I was eating them up. United were dominant in terms of possession, but they just couldn't break us down. We were only really in the game for a brief spell, but in that time Derek Wilkinson scored twice to give us a 2-0 win.

We were drawn to face Blackburn in the semi-finals of the cup and the tie was played at Manchester City's Maine Road ground. The game brought me up against the Northern Ireland centre forward Derek Dougan. He was a player who liked to dish it out and I always had a hard time against him. Derek was a big, tall lad who was all arms and legs. If you didn't use your arms against him, he'd knock you anywhere, but he could play as well.

Dougan scored the opening goal, but it should never have been allowed because he was well offside. Peter Johnson called me up, leaving Dougan there, so that he was blatantly offside when the ball was played up to him. But the linesman's flag stayed down and he carried on with his run before firing past Ron Springett. The referee allowed the goal to stand, which was unbelievable.

I was very upset at the injustice and my frustration boiled over when I clashed with Dougan. Tony Kay had gone in hard on Dougan and, as he was getting up, I whacked Derek in the stomach. Looking at both Kay and myself, Derek shook his head and said, 'I'll send you both a cup final ticket.' With Blackburn still leading, that made things worse for us because Dougan was taking the piss, saying that Blackburn were going to win. It annoyed me at the time, but all credit to the fella because when I look back, I have to chuckle and admit it was a brilliant thing to say after he had been hit.

Alan Finney had a goal ruled out when Derek Wilkinson was offside before Blackburn broke away to score a second goal. Ally McLeod played the ball down the right wing to Dougan who went through to score. John Fantham pulled a goal back with a header from a Tom McAnearney free-kick, but we couldn't force an equaliser. I certainly felt that we deserved a draw to force a replay.

We had been the favourites to win because Blackburn were struggling, but I couldn't understand our tactics that day. Harry Catterick told us to send long balls up to Keith Ellis, but Blackburn had a big raw-boned centre half called Matt Woods who had him in his pocket. Catterick never altered things, and of course we obeyed orders, but I think we'd have won the game if we'd played the ball on the ground more. Instead, we had to keep sending it up over the top to Keith and it just didn't work out.

People often say that to lose a semi-final is worse than losing in the final and I have to agree because it was so disappointing for us. At least you have the occasion of playing at Wembley or wherever if you get to a final, but there is no such experience in a semi-final. It would have been great for the Wednesday fans to have seen us at Wembley, but it wasn't to be.

Our League form dipped after that and we dropped down from third to fifth after winning just once in the last five games of the season. But we had more than con-solidated our First Division status and proved the doubters wrong, so it was a very good campaign.

On a personal note, it was my first full season in the top flight. I had established myself as a First Division player and been an ever-present in the side, playing in all 47 League and cup fixtures. I was therefore in a position to reflect on some hard-fought battles against various tough centre forwards.

One of the hardest players I faced was Andy Lochhead who played for Burnley. He was a big, raw-boned Scottish lad and you had to hit him hard. It was a battle with him all the time because he always came back once he'd been hit.

I never really had any trouble with Tottenham's Bobby Smith, but he was a battler who'd bundle a goalkeeper over when he had the chance. When we played Tottenham, especially when we were at White Hart Lane, Ron Springett would ask me to protect him because he was wary of the physical threat posed by Bobby. 'Don't let him come in,' he'd say. 'Stop him from hitting me.' So I had to try and stop Smithy charging in. The three of us knew each other well because we were England teammates and once, as we were waiting for a corner, I turned to Bobby and said, 'He's on about you again. He wants me to stop you going in, Bob, go and hit him.' The corner came over and it was Springett's ball, but Smithy went in as usual and knocked him straight over the line. He didn't get away with it though because the referee blew for a foul.

The first time I played at Bramall Lane, I faced the Sheffield United centre forward 'Doc' Pace. Doc was a good player, but he played like they do today and was always on the floor. He used his body well and, even when he wasn't being fouled, he made it look that way by going down for everything. Harry Catterick sat next to me before the game and explained what he wanted me to do. 'The referee is going to blow every time you tackle Doc and you're going to get booed, so go straight through him,' he said.

I followed Harry's instructions and kicked him off the park! I didn't bother which way he was turning, I just went in. The Bramall Lane crowd would have killed me if they could. The Blades' fans never forgot it and called me 'Mucky Duck' after that. I got on with Doc off the field and we'd drink together and have a good chat. He always used to call me a dirty bastard, but he was laughing when he said it!

What the United fans didn't know was that I had modelled myself on one of their heroes, Joe Shaw. Before I was in the team at Wednesday, I'd often go and watch Joe play for Sheffield United in midweek games. I'd stand on the terrace at Bramall Lane and keep a close eye on him. I picked up certain things from watching Joe because his anticipation was brilliant. How he read the game was unbelievable. Joe was only small for a centre half and he rarely headed the ball. The only time I remember Joe heading the ball was if he was in the clear, with no one putting him under pressure. Most of the centre forwards in his day were great big lads, so he didn't tend to go for the ball with them. He used to back off them and wait for the knock-on.

I played it hard, of course, but I would hit a centre forward fairly and wouldn't say I was a dirty player. I made plenty of fouls, but they weren't deliberate, unless they fouled me and then I would give as good as I got. My thinking was always, 'If that centre forward plays dirty on me, I'll play dirty on him.' We were taught to win the ball hard. When you were up against a feeble player, he'd be out of the game if you hit him hard, looking for you all the time. If they waited for you and hit you back, you knew you were in for a hard game. Supporters would boo me at away grounds, especially if I'd gone in hard on one of their favourite players, but that only geed me up. I used to love it because it made me feel ten feet tall and I felt it made me better as a player.

When the situation called for it, I would have a word with an opposition player to unsettle him. There would be times when I'd move across to the wing when a long ball had been played and I'd say to the winger, 'Come on, give me a run, let's see how fast you are.' It's amazing how it would put them off, allowing me to get the ball. I've got no doubt that sort of thing still goes on all the time in today's game.

The centre forwards were always big lads who never came off you. But then little players emerged like Ian St John at Liverpool and Blackburn's Roy Vernon who kept coming for short balls and using their pace, so you had to be on your toes all the time. Ray Pointer was also quick and he gave me some problems.

Another opponent I came up against was Brian Clough. I never found him any trouble at all to keep out. But you could have him under control for eighty-nine minutes and then he'd get a goal. He was that type of player. I can remember in one game he knocked the ball in and then laughed at me as he ran back, which really annoyed me. Cloughie would also be on at the referee, complaining all the time and asking for protection if you kicked him. But you couldn't take away from him the fact that he was a great goalscorer.

I used to love having a laugh and winding opposition players up. On one occasion when we played Tottenham, we were waiting for a corner to come over from Cliff Jones. I went behind Jimmy Greaves and pulled his shorts straight down. He didn't like it, but he didn't say anything until after the game when he called me a twat! Many years later, he came to Sheffield for an after-dinner speaking engagement at a dinner I attended. He didn't know I was there until I shouted, 'Don't forget to tell them about the shorts, Jimmy.'

I had another way of winding up centre forwards when we were waiting for a corner to be taken. With the referee taking up his position by one of the posts, I'd say loudly, 'Don't call the referee a bastard, number nine!'

'Don't worry Peter, I'm watching him,' the referee would reply.

Things went on in the game with players trying to psych each other out. Certain full-backs, for example, would say, 'Come past me once more and it's broke.' If the opponent was a shy type of character, he wouldn't go past him. That sort of thing no doubt happens in the current game. I can remember Peter Eustace being intimidated by West Brom's Derek Kevan soon after he had got into the first team as a young lad. He was a smashing bloke, Derek, but he was a big, rough lad who played it hard. During the match, Eustace shouted over to me, 'Swanny, he says he's going to break my leg.'

'Don't be frightened of him – break his,' I replied.

I probably used to go in harder on Derek Kevan than anyone else because I knew he'd come back. He once got hold off me by the scruff of the neck during a game after being upset by a challenge I'd made. 'You and me,' he growled, 'after the game.' I threw him off, carried on playing and after the game it was all over, with nothing more said.

The training routine was pretty much the same as when I was a part-timer, doing laps round the pitch. Then we went onto sprinting before finishing the session with a game. There's more ball work now but we did very little with the ball. Every player knows what does him good and I used to have my own personal routine. At the beginning of the week, after the training session had finished, I would go on the Spion Kop and run up to the top of it. I'd then walk down and run up again, repeating the exercise several times. It was a simple routine, but very effective because it built up my thigh muscles.

I was always a lean lad and my mum used to give me the best food to try and help me put weight on, but I was always around twelve stone. The fact that I didn't have much weight helped with my pace and in training, over a twenty-yard sprint, I was one of the fastest at the club. I stood at six foot and a quarter-inch tall, which is nothing compared to today's defenders. But I always looked taller than I was when I was in my kit, probably due to the rolled up shorts!

We never really thought about the food we were eating in those days. I'd eat a normal sort of diet during the week and then on Friday night I ate as much as I could before I went to bed. This was as a result of a professor telling us to eat a lot of starchy food the night before a game. He explained the starch would make glucose, so I'd go to bed bloated after stuffing myself! Whether it was psychological or not, I don't know, but I used to feel brilliant when I got out on the pitch and I could have run all day.

If we were playing at home, we'd meet up at the Grand Hotel in Sheffield for lunch. You could choose from steak, fish or eggs, with rice pudding as a sweet. I always had two poached eggs on toast. Glucose tablets were also passed round. Pasta was on the menu when I came back following the ban, but we didn't have it during my first spell.

I was never a big drinker when I was playing. I'd have a drink after a game, but we weren't allowed to drink after Wednesday night in the build-up to a game. At Christmas time, when we played on Christmas Eve, Christmas Day and Boxing Day, I'd go out with my wife Norma and my in-laws and I'd be sat there with a Coke or another soft drink. It was amazing to learn how many phone calls Harry Catterick received, telling him I'd been out drinking before a game. Fortunately, he believed it when I explained that I'd not been drinking alcohol. When I did go out for a drink, I'd often head out to pubs in Derbyshire rather than risk getting into any trouble in the centre of Sheffield. On the occasions when I did go out in Sheffield, there were times when Sheffield United fans would have a go at me. You would also get fans from other clubs who were staying in Sheffield after watching their team play. There would always be the type who wanted to cause trouble and have a pop at you. Once they'd had something to drink, they'd get a bit brave and start slagging you off. You have to try and keep your cool and turn away. It's the ones who can't turn away who get in trouble. There were odd occasions when I got involved in a fight, but nothing serious.

Some managers regularly played in five-a-sides because they thought they could still do it. And when players received the ball, they would often play it straight to the manager. It was just like when you were playing at school and lads passed the ball straight to the PE teacher. When I was in the Football League side under Joe Mercer, we were playing a five-a-side game in training one day when Joe decided to join in. When one particular player passed the ball to Joe, I shouted, 'Don't give the ball to him, he's playing from memory!' Joe looked over and stared at me. 'Be careful lad,' he said sternly. You had to be careful because no matter how good you are as a player, if a manager takes a dislike to you, then you can forget it because they'll try and get you out.

You didn't dare step out of line with Harry Catterick in charge. I can remember one occasion when I was called into his office along with Tony Kay. We'd just got in for training and Catterick came into the dressing room as we were about to get changed. 'You two, Kay and Swan, before you get stripped, I want you in the office,' he ordered. We both went to his office and it soon became clear that he wasn't happy. 'I'm getting phone calls and letters and there are people stopping me in the street, telling me about you two being out on the town on a Friday night.' We both told him it wasn't true – which was the case – and hoped he'd believe us. But we weren't expecting what came next, which summed up Catterick's tough handling of players. He said, 'I'm not bothered about what anybody tells me in phone calls or letters, but if you two don't do it for me on a Saturday, you'll get some of that [pointing to his clenched fist] and you'll never kick a ball again.'

Catterick was a hard man and I liked that type of man-ager because he'd give you a good bollocking when you needed it. He was quite a big guy who spoke with a lot of authority, so you didn't mess about. If you retaliated to a challenge, conceded a penalty or got sent off, he'd be into you. But when you'd had a good game, he would congratulate you, saying something like, 'Brilliant, you've done a good job today' or 'I thought you should have done this, but you've done things right and it worked out.'

I have a lot to thank Catterick for because he did so much for my game, turning me into an international player. He'd build me up before games by saying, 'You're the best centre half in England.' My elevation to the England side proved him right.

8

Three Lions on my Shirt

Representing your country is one of the greatest honours for a professional footballer and I was fortunate enough to play on the international stage.

My first taste of international football came when I played for the England Youth team against Holland in Arnhem, with the great Duncan Edwards skippering the side. I later made the step up to the Under-23 team, winning three caps at that level. Ron Greenwood, who later became England manager, was in charge of the Under-23s. Greenwood was very thorough in his approach, giving you a lot of tips on the opposition and how they played. He knew which side of bed the player you were facing got out of. I used to like managers like that. They'd sit next to you and tell you what type of player he was and what he liked to do, which meant you were fully prepared. There were some players who were so keyed up before a game that they forgot what they'd been told. But I always seemed to have it fixed in my mind which way the player was going to turn when he had his back away from me, so I found that in-depth analysis like that worked tremendously well for me.

Greenwood approached me on one occasion and said that if I didn't get a call-up for the next Under-23 international, I shouldn't worry about it because I'd be in the full squad for the game against Scotland at Hampden Park in April 1960. So when I wasn't included in the Under-23 squad, it looked as though I was set for a call up to the full squad. That appeared to be confirmed when Eric Taylor called me into his office at Hillsborough and said, 'You've got your first cap against Scotland.' But I didn't hear anything else, so I queried the situation with Eric. 'That's what they told me, Peter,' he said. What went off, I don't know, but Bill Slater of Wolves was in the side instead of me. Winterbottom was trying to find a settled back line following the retirement of the great Billy Wright a year earlier. Birmingham's Trevor Smith and Ken Brown of West Ham had both been tried in Wright's position before Slater got his chance.

I was disappointed at missing out on the Scotland game, but I didn't have to wait long to make my full England debut because I received a call-up later that month. I was named in the squad for the next game against Yugoslavia at Wembley on 11 May 1960 and was also included in the party for the trip to Spain and Hungary later in the month. I was called into Eric Taylor's office one day and given the news of my selection. 'There's the telegram Peter, you're in,' he said. The FA used to send a telegram to inform you of your call-up. The telegram also told you where you had to report and at what time. News of my selection for the squad appeared in the *Sheffield Morning Telegraph*. Basil Easterbrook wrote, 'Swan has played a leading part in his club's fine showing in the League and Cup this season, and in addition has turned in convincing performances in three Under-23 internationals.' Walter Winterbottom was the manager and he named me in the starting line-up to face Yugoslavia, as a replacement for Bill Slater. It turned out that Slater had been informed of the decision just a few minutes before being told he had been named Footballer of the Year. I was given Billy Wright's old no. 5 shirt in the following line-up: Springett; Armfield, Wilson, Clayton, Swan; Flowers, Douglas, Haynes, Bakers; Greaves, Charlton.

Yugoslavia took the lead when I was lured out of position, allowing an unmarked player called Galic to lift the ball over Ron Springett. We came back to lead 2-1 through goals from Bryan Douglas and Jimmy Greaves. Yugoslavia equalised and then Kosctic put them 3-2 up with ten minutes to go. But with just over a minute remaining, Joe Baker scored to make it 3-3. Baker talked with a Scottish accent because he was brought up there after being born in England, and had actually represented Scotland at schoolboy level. He played for Arsenal after spending some time in Italy with Torino.

I was very nervous and full of tension all through the game and I don't think I touched the ball more than four times. I was getting beaten to the ball and didn't even get any good defensive headers in. I'd never been like that in any game before. On that performance, I didn't think I'd get picked again because I felt that I hadn't done much right, to be honest. You know when you've played well and you don't need anyone to tell you when you've had a bad game. I was not the only one who struggled that day. Ronnie Clayton, who was the captain, also had a poor game. He had been a good wing half in his day, but he was getting on a bit by then. Basil Easterbrook, writing in the *Sheffield Telegraph*, commented:

Clayton's deflections were so great that even Billy Wright would have been struggling to close the gaps. I thought our troubles stemmed directly from Clayton, who gave one of the poorest performances ever seen from an England captain. Swan never had a real chance.

That proved to be Clayton's last appearance for England because he was dropped after that.

The following morning we flew to Spain, which was fortunate timing for me because if I hadn't got on tour, I might not have played for England again. Members of the travelling party were handed a booklet, detailing the itinerary for the trip. There was also a page of 'Special Notes For Players' which went under the signature of FA Secretary Sir Stanley Rous. In the section relating to fees and expenses it stated:

> All players will be allowed travelling expenses to and from London and will be given an allowance of £2 per day during the period spent abroad. Players will receive the following match fees: – Players £50; Reserves £30.

Going away with the squad helped me to settle into the England set-up. The pressure was off a little because we were away from our own supporters. I also got to know the other players better after spending so much time in their company and they all tried to make me feel at home.

Johnny Haynes replaced Clayton as captain for the game against Spain and Bobby Robson came into the side. Robson was a classy player who played the game fairly. I wasn't surprised at all to see how successful he became as a manager because he knew the game inside out. You'd listen to Bobby because he talked a good game – and still does, of course. Walter Winterbottom introduced a system with Bobby Robson and Ron Flowers inside. When we lost the ball, both players would tuck in and it made four across the middle. Peter Brabrook, who was a flying winger for Chelsea, also came into the side and that turned out to be his only appearance. He'd use his pace by knocking the ball past the full-back and chasing it. It had been raining in Madrid, so the ground was soft and slippery. I can remember Joe Baker struggling because he'd only taken a pair of football boots with moulded rubber studs, which were suitable for playing on hard surfaces, so he was slipping all over the place. It was disappointing because we lost 3-0 but, on a personal note, I felt more settled and played better as a result. Despite the fact that we conceded three goals, I knew I'd done okay and felt confident that I'd retain my place for the next game.

From Spain, we went to Hungary a week later. All the talk before the match was about the teenage Hungarian centre forward, Florian Albert, who was grabbing the headlines after some good performances. Manchester United's inside forward Dennis Viollett was included in the side for his debut. He was a player I didn't like to play against when we faced Manchester United because he was the type who came off you. I felt that I played him well, but until I really got into that way of thinking, I found him difficult. Fortunately, I had the pace to deal with the quick players. They used to time us in training at Sheffield Wednesday and I think I was the fastest off the line. We caused problems for the Hungarians, but we were let down by poor finishing. I had a good game against Albert, even though we lost 2-0 and he scored both goals. The next day, he was quoted as saying that I was the hardest centre half he'd come up against.

There were calls for the inclusion of Tottenham's Maurice Norman around this time, but Walter Winterbottom kept faith with me. Maurice was a lot bigger than me, probably about six feet four inches tall, so he was dominant in the air. Maurice was a good player, don't get me wrong, but I think the press were pushing for him to be included in the England side because he was at Spurs and there was perhaps a bit of southern bias.

When I collected my fourth cap against Northern Ireland in Belfast in October 1960, I can remember clashing with centre forward Billy McAdam at a set piece. He didn't bother with the ball as it came over, he just whacked me right across the chest. After that, when we faced each other in League games, I had no more trouble with McAdam because he always kept out of my way. He no doubt thought I was going to get my own back. I finished on the winning side for the first time as an England player, with Jimmy Greaves scoring twice in a 5-2 win. Bobby Smith, Bobby Charlton and Bryan Douglas were the other goalscorers. The twinning of Greaves and Smith was a sign of great things to come for both England and Tottenham. Jimmy was one of the best goalscorers I've ever seen. It was unbelievable how he knew which position to be in to score. It's a natural talent you can't coach.

We followed the Northern Ireland match with a World Cup qualifier in Luxembourg. Walter Winterbottom named an unchanged line-up. He had decided to keep a settled side, where possible, on the way to the 1962 World Cup finals. We beat Luxembourg 9-0 with hat-tricks for both Greaves and Bobby Charlton. Bobby Smith scored twice with Johnny Haynes the other goalscorer. As everyone knows, Bobby Charlton was a brilliant player. He could score a goal from anywhere because he'd got a hard shot and would regularly try his luck from way out. He also could play on either wing. As a lad, Bobby kept himself to himself because he appeared to find it difficult to mix. When you compare Bobby with his brother Jack, who admittedly I don't know all that well, they appear to be two different personalities altogether. You couldn't take anything away from Bobby as a footballer because he was brilliant, but when it came to a night out with the lads, he wanted his own way. Someone would say something like, 'Let's go to The Travellers' and he'd say, 'Oh no, I don't want to go to The Travellers, I want to go somewhere else.'

The rest of them generally went along with what Bobby wanted, so he usually got his way.

I felt at home playing for England by this time and it helped to have my Wednesday teammate, Ron Springett, in goal. We had a great understanding and I knew where he was without even looking. Ron commanded his area very well and would shout out instructions all the time. He'd shout, 'Keep your eye on him' or whatever was required.

Spain were our next opponents and we were out to avenge our defeat in Madrid earlier in the year. Alfredo Di Stefano, who was one of the all-time greats, was difficult to play against. I'd rate him as the best player I ever faced. He played as a centre forward, but he played deep. The only time you were really up against him man-to-man was when he came up for a free-kick or a corner. He'd be at the back of his front line and come up at the last minute. Fortunately, Di Stefano didn't give me much trouble that day. He was coming towards the end of his career at the age of thirty-three and wasn't as effective as he had been. It was a muddy pitch, just like it had been in Madrid, but we managed to master the conditions better than the Spaniards, putting some good passes together. Jimmy Armfield had a very good game, keeping the great winger Gento quiet. Spain twice came from behind to equalise, but we ran out 4-2 winners with Bobby Smith scoring twice.

Walter Winterbottom's policy of keeping a settled side worked well. He decided to keep all the players together, even playing us in the Inter-League games, to help us develop a good understanding. We also started having regular training sessions at various venues including Lilleshall. The policy paid dividends because we were knocking goals in at this time. Winterbottom was forced to make a change for the game against Wales following an injury to Ron Springett, who'd been hurt in an Inter-League match. Sheffield United's Alan Hodgkinson took over in goal. Greavsie gave us the lead after only two minutes and Wales never recovered from the early setback, conceding four more goals and scoring only once in reply. Goals were flowing freely for us with the five-goal blast taking our tally to an impressive 23 in 4 matches. If we thought our five-goal haul against Wales was good, better was to come in the following game against Scotland at Wembley.

Before the game, Scotland's Denis Law was quoted in the newspapers as saying that I was the weak link in the England side. That obviously made me determined to prove him wrong and I was 100 per cent focused on the match. Bobby Robson put us in front early in the game and Greavsie scored twice to put us firmly in charge. Scotland fought back to cut our lead to one goal at 3-2 early in the second half. But any thoughts of a Scotland come-back were ended when they were sunk by five goals in an eleven-minute spell. Johnny Haynes was superb, playing some killer passes and scoring twice. Greavsie grabbed a hat-trick and Bobby Smith scored twice in a memorable 9-3 victory. Ian St John was the Scotland centre forward and I had him in my shorts! I couldn't resist having a dig at the Scots after what had been said about me before the game. As we were leaving the field at the end of the match, I trotted over to have a word with Denis Law. 'Not bad for a weak link, am I?' I said. He just laughed it off. There's no doubting that Law was a very good player, but if he went into a tackle, he always went over the top. He'd have his foot up and that sort of thing could break your leg.

We enjoyed another comprehensive victory in the following game against Mexico at Wembley, despite being without the in-form Jimmy Greaves and Bobby Smith. Greavsie, who was on the verge of joining AC Milan, was suspended by Chelsea after refusing to go on a club tour while Smith was ruled out through injury. Gerry Hitchens made his debut and he got his international career off to a flying start, scoring after just ninety seconds. Hitchens was a good player for Aston Villa, but I found him easy enough to play against. We went on to win 8-0 with Bobby Charlton scoring a hat-trick.

We then faced Portugal in Lisbon in a World Cup qualifier. They had a towering centre forward called Torres who was about six feet eight inches tall. You'd stand behind him and not be able to see anything, but I came out on top against him. Ron Springett and Bobby Robson combined to gift Portugal the opening goal and it finished 1-1 with Ron Flowers scoring the equaliser from a free-kick late in the game. I knew him well because he was a Doncaster lad who came from Edlington and I'd played against him at school level. Ron was a brilliant player and I couldn't say anything bad about his game or his character. He was a big, strong lad who was equally good in the air and with his feet. It was very rare that he did anything wrong.

We went from Lisbon to Rome a few days later to face Italy and won 3-2, which was a tremendous result. The Italians were great players, but they were very 'mardy', as we say in Yorkshire. If you got the ball off them, they'd kick out. They'd spit at you as well. Gerry Hitchens gave us an early lead, but Italy hit back to go 2-1 up. Jimmy Greaves did well to set up Hitchens for the equaliser. Greavsie then scored the winner five minutes from time after getting on the end of a ball from Johnny Haynes.

I was Jimmy's roommate for England and we became good friends. He was a good laugh, joining in with everything we did as players and he was good for the team because you've always got to have characters to build up the morale. Jimmy had a twitch that made him look like he was nodding the ball in. When he twitched as he was talking, Ron Springett would pretend to dive for the imaginary ball! Jimmy of course went on to become a popular television pundit and yet, when I've watched him on television over the years, I've never seen him twitch. It surprised me when I later learned that Jimmy was an alcoholic because there was no sign of that when we were teammates. After a match with England, we'd have a few beers, but Jimmy was always on Coca-Cola. I don't know when the drinking started, but I'm glad that he came through his problems and enjoyed a successful career in the media. He still writes a column in *The Sun* and does regular after dinner-speeches.

We suffered a setback with a 3-1 defeat in Austria. It was our third game in seven days on tour and Walter Winterbottom decided to take a look at a couple of fringe players. Brian Miller, the Burnley centre half, came in as a replacement for Bobby Robson and Miller's Burnley teammate John Angus also played, taking the place of Mick McNeil.

There were several enforced changes for the World Cup qualifier against Luxembourg at Highbury. Johnny Haynes was injured while Jimmy Greaves and Gerry Hitchens were both on club duty in Italy. My Sheffield Wednesday teammate, John Fantham, made his debut and there were also places for Ray Pointer and Dennis Viollett. We struggled to get into our stride and were booed by the fans until Bobby Charlton scored two long-range efforts. Pointer and Viollett also got their names on the scoresheet in a 4-1 win.

The following game, against Wales at Ninian Park in October 1961, was a bruising encounter, with several players picking up knocks. I was involved as Wales took the lead on the half-hour mark. As I tussled with centre forward David Ward for the ball, my boot came off and Graham Williams took advantage of the situation, firing home as the ball ran free. Bryan Douglas equalised just before half-time as we secured a 1-1 draw. Douglas was a tricky little winger who we called 'The White Pygmy' because of his size. He was a Lancastrian who spent his whole career at his home-town club, Blackburn Rovers. Ray Wilson made his return to the side in the Wales game after a ten-match absence. Ray was a really nice fella and a brilliant player who of course went on to play in the 1966 World Cup-winning side. I'd rate him as one of the best players I ever played with.

The match against Portugal at Wembley later that month was a crucial match, with a place in the World Cup finals at stake. Portugal featured a teenage Eusebio and Walter Winterbottom told us before the game that we'd got to watch this highly rated young lad. Walter, who had seen him play, said he was a tremendous player and warned us not to give him too much room. It turned out to be good advice because Eusebio was brilliant that day and hit the woodwork twice. He was certainly one of the best players I ever faced. Goals from John Connelly and Ray Pointer early in the game gave us a 2–0 win to secure our passage to Chile.

The following month we played another Home Championship international against Northern Ireland at Wembley. I can't understand why they got rid of the Home Championship. I thought they were worthwhile games because they kept the team together and allowed the manager to experiment with different players. Walter Winterbottom used the game to try Ipswich Town's Ray Crawford alongside Johnny 'Budgie' Byrne of Crystal Palace in attack, who was making a name for himself in the Third Division. But they failed to gel really and we were lucky to avoid defeat, Bobby Charlton scoring in a 1–1 draw.

As we prepared to take on Austria at Wembley, I knew that I would be up against Johan Busek, who Walter Winterbottom rated as the most dangerous centre forward on the Continent at that time. Roger Hunt, who of course also featured in the 1966 World Cup-winning side, marked his debut with a goal. After we won 3-1 and I had managed to keep Busek under control, Winterbottom was quoted as saying, 'Peter Swan's performance against him [Busek] was particularly encouraging. I thought he had an excellent game against a very fine player.' Walter was brilliant on tactics and had a great knowledge of the game, but I thought he wasn't hard enough. I liked the type of manager who was forceful and imposed discipline. I loved Harry Catterick for that because you knew that if you made a mistake, you'd be in for a telling off. Walter was a schoolteacher type. He wouldn't exactly call you a naughty boy, but it was going along the same lines. You knew he was the gaffer and you wouldn't argue with him, but I felt he could have been harder.

When we played Scotland at Hampden Park in April 1962, they were obviously keen to avenge our 9-3 victory over them the previous year. I recall a clash between Denis Law and Stan Anderson. The ball had gone out for a goal kick and we were walking away from the penalty area as Ron Springett went to retrieve the ball. Law looked across at Anderson and was giving him abuse, saying that someone was shagging his wife or girlfriend, things like that. Anderson never even looked at Law and I was thinking, 'Well, if that was me, I'd have to smack him.' But it turned out that Anderson was merely biding his time, waiting to exact his revenge. The next time the ball went to Law, Anderson went straight through him. I conceded a penalty at the death, which was converted by Eric Caldow, as we suffered a 2-0 defeat. It was Scotland's first home victory over England since 1937.

Johnny Haynes, who took over the captaincy from Ronnie Clayton in only my second game for England, was a great leader. He was the type of captain who would bollock anybody. He'd get really wound up, always shouting and complaining on the field and having a go at the referee. Johnny would never shout anything complimentary to you while you were playing. But at the end of the game he'd come over and say, 'Well done Swanny, brilliant,' or whatever. I thought he was a good captain because he would drive you on. It was very rare that Johnny gave the ball away and he was good at playing a reverse pass, looking one way and sending the ball in the opposite direction. He was a nice lad who didn't get carried away with what he'd achieved, unlike some others. You get some people who forget where they were brought up. I would say eight out of ten footballers come from working-class backgrounds and it's laughable when they suddenly try to become posh.

My inclusion in the 1962 World Cup squad was noted in the match-day programme for Sheffield Wednesday's last match of the season against Burnley. The editorial said:

> Not everybody is enamoured with Peter. Some people would prefer a centre half-back of elegance. Our pivot, however, has shown the possession of the big match temperament and seeing that he has been an England regular for three seasons, the selectors have obviously been satisfied.

Our penultimate World Cup warm-up match against Switzerland at Wembley saw us win 3-1. But it was an unconvincing performance and only a brilliant display from Ron Springett kept Switzerland at bay. It turned out to be my final appearance for England after playing in 19 consecutive games.

We stayed in London that night, ready to fly out to Peru the following morning for the final warm-up game. I woke with flu-type symptoms and felt lousy. A doctor was called and he diagnosed tonsillitis. I think there was a debate over whether they would take me in that condition. Obviously I didn't want to miss out on playing in the tournament, so I made out that I was okay to travel. The decision was made to give me medication in the hope that I would make a quick recovery, so I was drugged up for the nineteen-hour flight. By the time the Peru match came round I was still weak, so Tottenham's Maurice Norman came in to take my place alongside Bobby Moore who was also making his debut. Norman had been brought into the squad and people were ribbing me, saying that as a London-based player, he would get in ahead of me. The talk among players and supporters was that you had a greater chance of being picked for England if you were with a southern club. I would laugh off the suggestion, but at the back of my mind was the question of whether Norman would be picked. As it turned out, I was confined to my sickbed for the whole of the tournament, so no decision had to be made.

I seemed to be okay by the time we travelled to our training camp in Chile. Our base was a place which was used as a holiday venue for copper miners. I've never stayed in a worse place in my life. The facilities were very poor and it was a bit of an eye-opener, to say the least. As footballers, we were used to staying in plush hotels and being treated like royalty; nothing was too good for us. But here we found ourselves staying in a wooden hut and sleeping in camp beds. It made it seem like a Boy Scouts' camp instead of a base for the World Cup finals. Needless to say, all the players complained about the standard of the accommodation. There were comments like, 'I'm not sleeping in that.' On the plus side, there was plenty of open space where we could train.

To help the players relax, we were allowed to attend a concert in a village hall near our base. I'm always up for a laugh, playing practical jokes and things, so I got up and danced with these flamenco dancers who were there to entertain us. I threw myself into the routine, swinging a scarf round my head and generally making a fool of myself, which you do when you're enjoying yourself. Without my knowledge, someone took photographs of me cavorting on stage and they appeared in a local newspaper back home. Unfortunately, my wife saw the pictures and wasn't best pleased to see me dancing with these girls! Alcohol wasn't to blame for my behaviour because all we were drinking was Coca-Cola. Many crates of Coca-Cola were taken on the trip because they were strict on not allowing us to drink alcohol. Of course there were times on trips when players nipped out and drank without the manager knowing, but not on this occasion.

Following my recovery from tonsillitis, I was laid low once again after picking up a dysentery bug. I suffered agonising sickness and diarrhoea, which I wouldn't wish on anyone because it was relentless. No matter what I ate, it came out one way or the other. I was in the hut for two or three days, where I was looked after by the Sheffield United goalkeeper Alan Hodgkinson, before being taken to hospital. All I could do was drink a lot of fluids and I lost about three stone in weight. I was put on a glucose drip in hospital and spent about a week there. I was suffering from dehydration and they told me that if I hadn't been put on a drip, it could have been really serious. It was just a basic hospital, not like the ones in England. I was in a room on my own and it was quite a lonely experience. But it didn't really bother me that much because all I wanted to do was sleep. I phoned home and told my wife that I'd been suffering from sickness, but I didn't tell her how serious it was. Norma then read in the newspapers that I was in a bad way, so it was a worrying time for my family. England did not have a team doctor travelling with the party at that time, so I was in the hands of the local medics. My problems prompted the FA to take their own medical staff on trips abroad after that.

Bobby Robson and Bobby Smith also missed out on play-ing in Chile. Robson was injured and that was also the official reason for Smith's absence. I wasn't convinced that 'Smithy' was left out through injury though. I thought it was just an excuse from Walter Winterbottom for leaving him out of the squad. Whatever the reason, Smithy's absence was a crushing blow because he played a prominent part at that time. Just about every team we played were frightened of him because he was a tank-like player who caused problems for defenders. He'd had a good season for Tottenham and in the training camps all the foreign players were asking about him. With Smithy unavailable, Alan Peacock and Gerry Hitchens com-peted for the centre forward role. They were good players, but they weren't as effective as Bobby. Hitchens had secured a move to Inter Milan the previous year following a good performance for England in Rome. He soon adapted to the Italian game, playing the way they do over there. Like John Charles, who also played in Italy, Hitchens would fall over at the slightest challenge.

England reached the quarter-finals in Chile, suffering a 3-1 defeat at the hands of Brazil who went on to win the tournament. It was a big disappointment only to reach the last eight because many observers had fancied our chances of going all the way. In my view, Walter Winterbottom made a crucial error in the build-up to the tournament. He kept a fairly settled side together for two years and there was a good understanding among the players. But then, all of a sudden, he started changing the team around. Players who hadn't played for England before were brought in for important games. That seemed wrong to me after we'd been together for such a long time. I couldn't understand why he did that and I think other players felt the same.

Alf Ramsey, who succeeded Winterbottom, phoned me at home soon after taking over as England manager. He wanted to explain why I had been left out of his first squad. 'Don't worry, Peter,' he said, 'you're at the top of my list, but I'm looking at various players and trying different systems because I want to know what I've got.' I was in the squad once under Ramsey, when England played France at Hillsborough. But then I was banned before I could be picked again.

People say I would have played in the 1966 World Cup-winning team instead of Jack Charlton if it hadn't been for the ban. It has been said to me many, many times and I get sick of hearing it, to be honest. I suppose it's nice to hear it in a way because people mean it as a compliment, but at the same time I do get fed up with it. I think I would have been in the squad, but whether I'd have been in the team is another matter. I can't say that I'd have definitely been in the 1966 side if I'd have been available. I could have been injured or suffered a loss of form. It should also be remembered that different managers have their own ideas about players, so it is by no means certain that I would have been picked. Jack Charlton was a good, no-nonsense centre half, but I think I was a bit classier and played more football than him. At the same time, I could play it hard like Jack. But you have to give him his due and say that he did a very good job for England.

I have to admit it was a difficult time for me when England beat West Germany to win the World Cup in 1966. I watched the final on television and when the players were celebrating after the match, I couldn't help thinking, 'That could have been me.' I think it was only natural I felt that way after being a fixture in the side four years earlier. It was even harder for my old mate Jimmy Greaves, who had been an automatic choice until being injured and then found himself left out. He must have been devastated. I was disappointed for Jimmy, but Alf Ramsey must have seen something in Geoff Hurst, who of course went on to be the hero with a hat-trick in the final. Hurst's performance surprised me because he was the easiest player to play against. He never gave me any problems when I played against him. But all credit to him for his part in England's finest hour; you can never take that away from him. It is just a pity I wasn't able to share in the glory.

9

League Runners-up

My career was on the up and up as the start of the 1960/61 season loomed. With a place in the England side secured, I was also part of a Sheffield Wednesday side who had become a force to be reckoned with under Harry Catterick. Buoyed by our fifth-placed finish the previous term, we had high hopes of enjoying another good season.

When we reported back for the start of pre-season training, Catterick explained that he had drawn up a training schedule with trainer Tom Eggleston. He told us that we had to treat the training seriously and make every effort to improve our skills, with the emphasis on ball control. The training facilities we had were fairly basic. We had to change at the ground and walk a mile or so to the training ground on Middlewood Road, which is still used by Wednesday.

Catterick added to his backroom staff by bringing in Maurice Lindley as an assistant trainer. The pair knew each other from their time together at Everton and Lindley had managed Crewe and Swindon. I talked a lot to Maurice because he'd been a centre half and, although he wasn't involved with the first team, we exchanged views and he'd offer advice.

The training under Catterick was very different to when Eric Taylor was in charge because he was much more thorough in his approach. Before Catterick came to the club, all we did was lapping and sprinting, finishing off with a game of football. There was no work on set pieces or anything like that. Taylor would just tell us to go out and enjoy ourselves before a game, but Catterick would talk to players individually and tell them what he wanted them to do. He would also give you information about the opposition, telling you if the player you were facing had a particular trick he liked to use.

We worked a lot on set pieces and tactics under Catterick. I was part of a 'swivel' formation at the back, with Tom McAnearney and Tony Kay providing cover. If one of them was attacking on one side, the other would stay back, more or less in the centre of the park. That meant we were never caught flat.

Before that we were square at the back, making it easier for a winger to race on to a through ball. The new system introduced by Catterick meant we were more flexible.

Wednesday officials arranged an ambitious pre-season tour of the Soviet Union in the build up to the new campaign. A three-match programme behind the Iron Curtain was arranged and it proved to be an unusual experience. We went to Moscow where we were followed everywhere by members of the KGB. There was no nightlife either, so we couldn't really relax as we did at home. You felt you couldn't do anything and I was glad to get away from the place because it was a little intimidating.

We played CSKA at the Central Lenin Stadium in front of a crowd of over 50,000 and lost 1-0. From there we went to Georgia to play Dynamo. The facilities in the hotel we stayed at were very basic and there wasn't even any hot water. We suffered a 1-0 defeat again before heading back to Moscow for a game against Locomotiv, which we lost 3-2.

It was a fairly punishing schedule due to the travelling, but we were young lads, full of energy, so it wasn't a problem.

Ron Springett continued to live in London, training at his old club QPR and travelling up to Sheffield the night before a game. He'd signed for Wednesday on the understanding that he would be able to remain in London and everyone was happy with the arrangement. Ron was a good mate of mine: we were in the England side together and developed a great understanding. If he missed the ball and I was there to head off the goal line, he'd turn round and say, 'Thanks Swanny, I knew you'd be there.' There were plenty of times when he came to my rescue as well.

Johnny Quinn was given a surprise call-up for the opening-day game against West Brom. Johnny was a good player who started out as a centre forward as a young lad before being switched to midfield. Ronnie Allen, who later managed West Brom, led the Albion attack. He was a nippy player, but I had him in my shorts that day and we won 1-0 following a goal from Bobby Craig. That was followed by a 1-0 win at Cardiff, with Alan Finney scoring the winner.

Norman Curtis ended his ten-year association with Wednesday when he signed for Doncaster. After giving Wednesday sterling service, featuring in four promotion-winning teams, Norman was deservedly rewarded with a benefit match and received £1,000, which was a lot of money in those days.

Our good start to the season continued and we retained second place after winning 2-0 at Cardiff at the end of August. We maintained our unbeaten start to the season with a good run during September, winning four games and drawing twice. That was despite uncertainty surrounding the future of Harry Catterick after Nottingham Forest declared interest in appointing him as their new manager. Forest, who were struggling at the foot of the First Division table, announced that they had offered the job to Catterick.

Responding to the reports, Catterick stressed that he hadn't applied for the post.

I think it would have been a step down for him because Forest were no way near as big as Wednesday. And despite winning two European Cups under Brian Clough, that remains the case to this day. Apart from anything else, I think Harry only had it in his mind to return to his old club Everton, which he eventually did, because they were his first love. It was an uncertain time because the situation dragged on for a couple of weeks before Forest were informed that Catterick would remain at Hillsborough, despite apparently being offered more money to go to the City Ground.

Burnley were the reigning League Champions and they visited Hillsborough towards the end of September. Burnley were a top side then, which is hard to believe for younger people now as they've been out of the top flight for so long. They had some good players like Ray Pointer, Jimmy McIlroy and Jimmy Adamson, with Adam Blacklaw in goal. Pointer was a centre forward who always showed a good turn of pace. He was the type of player you could keep out of the game for eighty-nine minutes, only to see him score in the last minute. Keith Ellis and Billy Griffin scored in the opening quarter of an hour to put us 2-0 up. Jimmy Robson pulled a goal back for Burnley, but John Fantham scored to seal a 3-1 win. England selector Harold Shentall was in the crowd and he must have been satisfied with my performance because I was subsequently named in the next England squad.

By the end of September, Wednesday and Tottenham were the only teams with unbeaten records in the whole of the Football League. Before we played Blackpool at Hillsborough in mid-October, there was much talk over whether the great Stanley Matthews would play. People used to say, 'Stanley never plays in Sheffield', but that was without foundation because he actually played in the city as often as he did elsewhere. Matthews remained a big attraction, even at the age of forty-five, so Eric Taylor had a word with the Blackpool manager to find out whether he would be playing. After being informed that Matthews definitely would be playing, Taylor leaked the news to the press, knowing that confirmation of his appearance would swell the gate. That was just one example of how canny Taylor was. Matthews did quite well early in the game, but faded as it went on. He was still tricky, but I think he'd carried on a bit too long. We beat Blackpool comfortably, with Keith Ellis scoring twice in a 4-0 win. Another clean sheet meant we had conceded only 7 goals in our opening 12 games.

Our 12-match unbeaten run came to end, however, when we crashed to a 4-1 defeat at Wolves in the following game. Wolves, who had finished runners-up to champions Burnley the season before, were 3-0 up after twenty-eight minutes. I was at fault for the third goal when I miskicked in front of goal and the ball went to Eddie Clamp whose shot beat the unsighted Ron Springett. It was game to forget for me because I also collided with Tony Kay, damaging his right shoulder, which had been broken in a car accident six weeks previously. Instead of going off, Kay had the shoulder strapped and carried on playing. A scan later revealed that he had suffered a broken collarbone.

We then returned to winning ways with a 2-0 win over Bolton, Keith Ellis scoring his 8th goal in 7 games. My good form led to inclusion in the Football League side for a game against our Italian counterparts at the famous San Siro stadium in Milan and that was a fantastic experience. I lined up alongside the likes of Denis Law, Johnny Haynes, Ron Flowers and Jimmy Armfield. I recall it being quite a rough game with some strong challenges going in. Ron Springett was knocked out in a goalmouth scramble and had to be replaced by Manchester City's German keeper

Bert Trautmann. Legendary Welsh centre forward John Charles was in the Italian team and I can remember making a good interception from him. I was a big admirer of John, who was a great player, but I was disappointed with the way he played that day. After he'd moved from Leeds to Italy to play for Juventus, you only had to touch him and he'd be over. Every time I challenged him in the game, he went down. I couldn't understand why he felt he had to do that because he was a giant of a fella.

With Springett having suffered concussion in Italy, he missed Wednesday's next game at Manchester United, leading to a call-up for Roy McLaren. Roy was a good keeper, but he wasn't in the same class as Ron. It was a goal-less draw at Old Trafford and we then faced leaders Tottenham at Hillsborough. Tottenham, who were unbeaten, had a seven-point lead over us. But a crowd of over 56,000 saw their impressive run come to an end. After Billy Griffin opened the scoring, Maurice Norman equalised and John Fantham struck the winner to give us a memorable 2-1 win.

The Spurs players took the defeat badly. Apparently, when Griffin went to shake hands with one of them at the end of the game, his offer was ignored and when he turned away, he was kicked on the ankle. I picked up a muscle strain during the match, forcing me to withdraw from a Sheffield representative side for a game in Glasgow. But I did enough to impress *Sheffield Star* journalist Fred Walters who praised my performance:

> I should rate this as Swan's finest display since he came into the Wednesday team. It was because of him that [Bobby] Smith was never really in with a chance.

Around that time, I was hailed by an Italian football magazine as 'truly one of the world's great centre halves'.

When a team is doing well and confidence is high, everyone wants the ball and things come naturally to players. It's amazing how many players hide when it turns the other way and results aren't going well. They would get in a little hole and you wouldn't see them. They wouldn't be the same confident player they'd been before. Fans often also single out players for criticism, sometimes when they don't deserve it. It can be hard for a player to shake it off once they've been made a scapegoat, even if they refuse to hide.

Tom McAnearney was like that. No matter how badly he was playing, Tommy always wanted the ball and never shirked his responsibility. When he played as a wing half, Tommy would always be trying to play balls which would cut the other team apart instead of playing short, safe passes. The passes Tommy tried would often go astray or get picked up by the opposition and the fans would then get on to him. When he played in an established half-back line in the Catterick era with myself and Tony Kay and things were going well, the fans loved him. Before that, Tommy received a lot of stick, but all credit to him because he would never hide. Tommy's brother Jim also played for Wednesday and was a good inside forward, with a lot of skill, but he lacked pace. Their younger brother Jack followed them down from Dundee, but he only made the reserves.

Following the euphoria of beating Spurs, we were soon brought crashing back down to earth with three successive defeats. We lost against Leicester and Aston Villa – both by a 2-1 scoreline – and then went down 4-2 at Everton. After edging to a 5-4 win over Blackburn, we drew at West Brom before facing Arsenal at Hillsborough on 23 December. Johnny Quinn gave us the lead and Terry Neill, who went on to manage Arsenal, marked his debut with an equalising goal soon afterwards to force a draw.

It also finished 1-1 in the return fixture at Highbury on Boxing Day, with Keith Ellis scoring our goal. Taking a point from a strong Arsenal side was no mean feat and we were in high spirits as we boarded the coach and prepared to head north. It turned out to be a trip none of us would ever forget, with an accident tragically ending a young player's career before it had even begun.

We were in the mood to celebrate on the way home; the drink was flowing and there was plenty of laughter. As usual, some of the lads were playing cards and others were chatting or enjoying a sing-song. Joining in the singing was a young Scottish inside forward by the name of Doug McMillan. He was only nineteen and had yet to break into the first team. It was regular practice for a youngster to travel with the first team to an away game, in order to give them valuable experience of mixing with senior players.

We joined the A1 and were heading on the Great North Road at Huntingdon when disaster struck. The driver appeared to lose control of the vehicle and it veered off the road, with the squeal of the breaks followed by a thunderous crash as the coach struck a bridge. That was the last thing I can remember before coming round and finding myself trapped between some mangled seats, with the coach on its side. Try as I might, I just couldn't free myself and others were also clearly in pain among the wreckage, groaning and calling out for help. Shards of glass and twisted metal made for a scene of devastation.

I was quickly freed from the wreckage after helpers arrived, but McMillan wasn't so lucky. He had been singing into a microphone at the front of the coach and was trapped alongside Johnny Quinn. While Quinn was helped free, it soon became clear that it would not be so easy to release McMillan. Fortunately, as fate would have it, a surgeon had been travelling behind the coach and was quickly on the scene. After all attempts to free Doug from the wreckage ended in failure, the surgeon realised that his life was in danger due to the lack of circulation. He told Doug that he would have to remove the trapped leg. Doug pleaded with him to save his leg, but he was told that the limb would have to be amputated in order to save his life. With precious time running out, the surgeon performed an amputation on the teenager's shattered right leg.

The amputation was just below the knee joint, so when Doug was later fitted with a false leg, you could hardly tell. All the players visited Doug regularly in hospital when he was recovering, helping to keep his spirits up. It must have been a devastating thing for the lad to see his dreams of a career as a professional footballer ended in such a cruel way. Dougie was a smashing lad and I think he would have made it as a pro. A benefit match for Doug was staged at Hillsborough, featuring various stars including Billy Wright and Bobby Charlton in a select XI and I was pleased to see a good crowd turn out. I've not heard of Doug for a long time, so I don't know how things turned out for him after the accident.

I suffered a double fracture of my left shoulder in the accident and the injury kept me out of action for a couple of months. Trainer Tommy Eggleston told me that he saw me thrown through the air by the impact of the vehicle hitting the bridge. I went to hospital and my arm was put in a sling to aid the healing process. But I was impatient and wanted to use my arm, so I regularly used to take it out of the sling, incurring the wrath of the nurses, who played hell with me! As a result of my impatience, the bones failed to knit properly and there is still a noticeable bump.

After just under two months on the sidelines, I made my comeback in a midweek home game against Nottingham Forest, playing with a good strapping on both shoulders and it seemed to do the job because I got through it. The bones had knitted, but I was in a bit of pain because they were still weak. I was also a bit apprehensive about the possibility of falling on my shoulder. I managed to knock the referee, Jack

Kelly, right off his feet with a powerfully struck shot! As usual, when that sort of things happens to a match official, Kelly's misfortune was met by a loud cheer from the crowd, but journalist Fred Walters failed to see the funny side of the incident. 'It is difficult to see what amusement some spectators at professional football matches derive from such occurrences as these,' he wrote in the *Sheffield Star*. Kelly had to be helped to his feet by our trainer Tom Eggleston before carrying on. We beat Forest 1-0 with a goal from Alan Finney whose cross was misjudged by keeper Peter Grummitt and the ball looped over him. I don't think I went on a pitch away from home without being jeered and, for some reason, the Nottingham Forest fans always gave me a lot of abuse. But the more abuse I received from the crowd, the more it raised my game. I thought it was brilliant, so I used to go over to the home fans and more or less thank them for booing me.

We were in third place, nine points behind leaders Tottenham, going into the match at home to Chelsea at the end of February. Alan Finney was the match-winner again, beating a young Peter Bonetti in the visitors' goal for the only goal of the game.

Next up was an FA Cup quarter-final tie at home to Burnley. I appreciated that Harry Catterick was faced with a selection dilemma because Ralph O'Donnell had done well as my replacement during the cup run. We had knocked out Leeds in the third round and then thrashed Manchester United 7-2 in a replay at Old Trafford before beating Leyton Orient to set up the clash with Burnley. Ralph had played in all four games and I realised that it would not be easy for Catterick to choose between us, especially as I was still struggling to regain match fitness. I decided to tell Catterick that I fully appreciated the difficulties he faced over selection, adding that if he decided against selecting me, I would accept the judgment in the proper spirit for the benefit of the team. Catterick and O'Donnell both appreciated the gesture. Ralph had taken a similar view when I won an immediate recall after proving my fitness. Despite playing very well in an unbeaten run of eight League and cup games, Ralph accepted that it was only right I should have my place back.

It has to be said, however, that not everyone was happy to be see me back in the team. I received one or two poison pen letters around this time, criticising me and saying that Ralph should be playing instead of me. One anonymous letter writer said, 'Now, Swanee, why don't you break the other shoulder and let O'Donnell play?' It was not the first time I had received poison pen letters. I'd had one before the FA Cup semi-final the previous season, but I don't know whether they were written by the same person. I was annoyed, but the letters didn't particularly worry me personally because I took the view that they were the work of cranks. My wife was upset by them, however, which I suppose was only natural. I didn't believe they were from genuine Sheffield Wednesday fans, but you never know because you can easily upset supporters if they favour certain players.

Harry Catterick voiced his anger over the letters in the local press, describing them as 'pitiful'. He added that some players would be upset by negative correspondence, but pointed out that they had the opposite effect where I was concerned, merely making me mad. Ralph O'Donnell was also full of sympathy, offering his support, after learning that I had received a letter calling for his inclusion as my replacement. Like me, Ralph was from South Elmsall and we got on very well. He was a really nice fella and I couldn't say a wrong word about him. Ralph was an educated lad who worked as a schoolteacher, playing part-time for Wednesday. At a time when the maximum wage at Wednesday was £20 a week, he received £16 as a part-timer. Coupled with his salary from teaching, he'd have earned some good money.

Catterick decided to pick O'Donnell ahead of me for the quarter-final game against Burnley, which ended in a goal-less draw. Ralph retained his place for the replay – which we lost 2-0 – and also played in the following League game at home to Wolves. With hindsight, I probably came back from injury a little too early and I think Catterick recognised this. I had wanted to return to playing as quickly as possible, even though I wasn't fully fit.

I was recalled for the game at Blackpool and had a good game against Ray Charnley. He was a tall and fairly lean centre forward who won one England cap. John Fantham scored the only goal of the game to give us the points.

Tottenham continued to dominate at the top of the table, but we seemed assured of at least the runners-up spot before another game in Lancashire, against Bolton. Fantham was the match-winner again with the solitary goal of the game.

We were always on the coat-tails of Spurs who had a great side. Danny Blanchflower, their kingpin in the middle of the park, was a brilliant player. They had a very hard player in Dave MacKay who was a tremendous competitor. Among the other key players for them were Alan Gilzean and John White, who was tragically killed a few years later after being struck by lightning on a golf course.

With an unbeaten League run since 3 December, we were keeping the pressure on Spurs ahead of Manchester United's visit to Hillsborough. The United side included Shay Brennan, Noel Cantwell, Maurice Setters, Bill Foukes, Nobby Stiles, Albert Quixall and Bobby Charlton, so it was a strong line-up, but we still managed to win 5-1 with Gerry Young scoring a hat-trick.

Our winning run continued with a 1-0 victory at Newcastle following a goal from Bobby Craig. Wales international Ivor Allchurch was the Newcastle centre forward. We faced each other a few times, both at club and international level. He was good on the ground rather than a bustling type of centre forward. The English game had been all about having a big centre forward who was strong in the air and after being used to facing that type of player, I found it quite difficult at first to defend against the smaller, ball-playing centre forwards when they started coming into the game. They came off you and, until I got used to facing them, I struggled to cope. I didn't know whether to go with the player or stay off him. But then your footballing brain kicks in and you learn how to handle the different style of play. West Ham's John 'Budgie' Byrne was one of the smaller players who caused problems for me. He was pacy and would come off you very quickly.

Our title challenge was still very much alive at Easter and we knew it was probably going to be a make-or-break time for us. Unfortunately, we could only draw 1-1 at Blackburn and it was the same result at home to Newcastle two days later, seriously affecting our chances of overhauling Tottenham at the top.

Amid speculation surrounding the future of Harry Catterick, we were held to a third successive draw at home to Leicester. A national newspaper report claimed that Catterick was preparing to quit at the end of the season after the Wednesday board failed to honour promises made to him when he turned down an approach from Nottingham Forest earlier in the season. Catterick was said to be critical of spending restrictions placed on him. He had wanted to sign centre forward Joe Baker from Hibernian, who was available for a small fee, but the board refused to sanction the deal. Catterick was trying to build a squad and obviously felt that Baker would be a very useful addition, but he couldn't persuade the board to give him the money to make the signing. That was very disappointing for Catterick and he made his feelings known. To add to the problems behind the scenes at Hillsborough, Catterick and general manager Eric Taylor weren't seeing eye to eye and there was a bit of friction between them. All we knew as players was hearsay because they didn't show there was anything wrong in front of us, but it is safe to say that their relationship was not as good as it could have been.

After Wednesday chairman Dr Andrew Stephen issued a statement, denying that spending restrictions had been placed on Catterick, the game against Leicester proved to be Harry's farewell as his departure was announced the following Monday. Catterick made no comment on the events leading up to his exit from Hillsborough, but he was quoted as saying that he felt quite happy to have fulfilled his promise when we won the Second Division champion-ship and 'put an end to the yo-yo business' – a reference to Wednesday's habit of bouncing between the top two divisions prior to his arrival.

We were shocked by Catterick's resignation because everybody liked him and respected him. Rather than tell us collectively that he was leaving, we were called into Catterick's office individually. When it was my turn to go in and see him, he wished me all the best and told me that he'd be coming back to get me. I had a good relationship with him, so it was no surprise really when he indicated that he'd like to sign me when he was at another club. It was no surprise either when Catterick went back to Everton soon afterwards, following the sacking of Johnny Carey. It had no doubt been pre-arranged, even though Catterick claimed he had no club to go to when he quit Wednesday. He'd played for Everton and was always talking about the old days when he was a player at Goodison, so I think it had always been his ambition to go back there as manager.

Eric Taylor took charge of the side on a temporary basis following Catterick's departure. Eric, who had of course been manager prior to Catterick's arrival, was a brilliant administrator, but he knew nothing about football, in terms of coaching or how to motivate a team. He couldn't come up to me before a game and tell me what I had to do. Catterick would sit down next to you and explain what he wanted you to do or he would tell the team collectively what he was looking for. But Eric's message before a game would still be, 'Go out and enjoy yourself.' I can't remember him ever telling me how he wanted me to play. During his first spell in charge, Taylor had adopted long-ball tactics. I couldn't play a short ball to someone like Tony Kay because I was expected to launch the ball forward at the earliest opportunity. Taylor's theory was that if you played the ball into the opposing penalty area a hundred times, you'd be certain to score, so we played a direct style. Things were different when Taylor took over from Catterick though because he carried on with the style of play that had been successful under Harry.

Our first game after the managerial upheaval was away at Tottenham and we lost 2-1, effectively ending any hopes we had of winning the title. We then prepared for a home game against Everton, pitching us against Catterick just twelve days after he had left Hillsborough. He received quite a hostile reception from the Wednesday fans, as often happens when someone returns to their former club. Frank Wignall replaced Alec Young in the Everton forward line because Young had been called up to represent the Army in a game. Wignall scored both goals for Everton as they won 2-1. The winner came following a misunderstanding between me and Peter Johnson. Billy Bingham, who later managed Northern Ireland, sent over a cross and I left it to Johnson, thinking he was going to clear. Unfortunately, he also thought I had the situation in hand and that left Wignall with a simple opportunity to score.

Catterick made a raid on Hillsborough later in the year when he signed Tony Kay. He didn't come back for me, however, despite saying that he would do when he left

Wednesday. I think he probably assessed his squad and decided that with a young Brian Labone there, he didn't need a centre half. Perhaps if Labone hadn't been there, he would have made a bid for me. Despite being happy at Wednesday, I would have been interested in a move to Everton. It would have been an honour to have received an offer from a big club like that. No matter how much you love a club, you have to remember that a career as a footballer doesn't last long, so it makes sense financially to move around. My wife Norma didn't want to leave Sheffield, so there would have been a lot of soul searching if Everton had come in for me, but there was no decision to be made in the absence of an offer.

We beat Chelsea 2-0 in the penultimate game of the season to move back into second place and to be sure of claiming the runners-up spot we had to win at Aston Villa on the last day. We suffered a 4-1 defeat at Villa Park, but Wolves failed to take advantage of our slip-up and we finished a point above them. Billy Griffin scored our consolation against Villa after telling everyone on the way to the match that he would get a goal. It was a disappointing end to the campaign. Our record following Harry Catterick's resignation was very poor, losing 3 out of 4 games.

After Spurs won the League and cup 'double', opponents had to be found for them in the Charity Shield. It was decided that an 'FA XI' would be assembled and I was part of that team. It was essentially an England team, but the FA didn't want to pay players the going rate for an international match. The England match fee at that time was £50, but we got the princely sum of £10 for playing in the Charity Shield, saving the FA around £500 by not being called an England side!

The Wednesday board appointed Vic Buckingham, who had been with Dutch club Ajax, as Catterick's replacement. Prior to his spell in Holland, Buckingham had managed Bradford and West Brom. Having worked abroad, Buckingham introduced foreign ideas to Hillsborough. After we had previously concentrated on our fitness in training, Buckingham got us to work with the ball all the time. After winning the opening three games of the 1961/62 season, we then won just once in seven games. If we could have played how Buckingham wanted us to play, all would have worked well. But I think the mistake he made was to try and change our style overnight, which was asking too much, in my opinion.

Buckingham was so far ahead in his thinking that he wanted us to play like they do today. He'd try to get Keith Ellis, who was a big, bustling centre forward, to lay the ball off. That was not Keith's style because he was a gangly lad who lacked finesse. Keith's strength was in the air and I think Buckingham was trying to get him to play in a way which didn't suit him. If I broke up an attack in my half, I had always knocked the ball long, but Vic wanted me to play the ball out instead. You could play a long ball on occasions when you found yourself under pressure, but otherwise it had to be played out.

Buckingham also had a more relaxed style of man-management than Harry Catterick. Whereas Catterick would give you a good bollocking if he felt you deserved it, Buckingham couldn't do that. I think a manager should be able to read the different personalities in his team, so that he can deal with each individual in the right way. Some need to be taken on one side and spoken to properly while others respond better to a real good, hard bollocking. Wednesday's Colin Dobson, for example, would go into his shell if he received a good telling off. He'd be finished if that happened, so the manager needed to sit next to him instead and build him up.

Buckingham was a flamboyant character who used to flick the brim of his trilby hat when he put it on. He'd sit on the edge of the table in the dressing room and flick his trilby so that it tilted to the back of his head. When we went down to play in London, there was always one of his showbiz friends coming into the dressing room. They'd say, 'Hello Vic, how are you?' and he would greet them with a kiss, whether they were male or female. We players weren't used to that sort of theatrical behaviour and we'd look at each other and say, 'He's a fucking poof, he's definitely queer.' He wasn't, it was just his way.

We always went to a show on the Friday night if we were playing in London and Buckingham would take us backstage at the end to meet the stars. I remember after one performance meeting Leslie Crowther who appeared on television at the time in the *Black and White Minstrel Show* and *Crackerjack*. 'Hello Pete, how are you?' he said.

'My kids think you're marvellous,' I replied. With the rest of the lads looking on, I couldn't resist adding, 'I think you're crap, but the kids think you're marvellous.'

On another occasion, Buckingham took us to meet Lulu. We also had a chance meeting with Roger Moore at Rome airport. He was starring in the television series *Maverick* at the time before appearing in *The Saint* and of course playing the part of James Bond. The lads couldn't work out at first whether it was him or not, so I went up to him and introduced myself. 'Excuse me, it is Roger Moore, isn't it? I'm not an autograph hunter, we're a football team.' After confirming that he was indeed Roger Moore, he told me to bring the rest of the players over and he was brilliant, having a good chat with us, telling us a bit about his lifestyle. Apparently, after filming had finished, they would have a big party which could go on for a week, eating, sleeping and shagging. Nice work if you can get it!

The trip to Rome came when we played AS Roma in the second round of the Fairs Cup. Gerry Young scored a hat-trick as we took a 4-0 lead in the first leg at Hillsborough. We lost 1-0 in the return leg when I scored an own goal. Tony Kay had a running battle with Roma's inside forward in that game. Tony was a hard player who never shirked anything and the Italians didn't like it. After being attacked by several Roma players as he left the pitch, Kay accused them of 'gangsterism'. We faced Barcelona in the quarter-finals of the Fairs Cup. After winning 3-2 at home in the first leg, we went out of the competition after losing 2-0 in front of a 75,000 crowd in Spain.

When we were on an away trip for a weekend fixture, we were allowed to have a couple of halves of bitter on a Friday night and were told we had to be back at the hotel for 11.30 p.m. One thing that Buckingham didn't like was players having breakfast in bed, insisting we had to get up and have it in the dining room.

We experienced a run of 3 defeats in 4 games in April, which prompted some to question Buckingham's managerial ability. The poor sequence of results began with a heavy defeat at Tottenham. The Spurs players were expected to be jaded after playing against Benfica in the European Cup a few days before. But they made a mockery of that assumption with Jimmy Greaves scoring twice as they thrashed us 4-0.

Morale was low at Hillsborough around this time because we were in tenth place, only four points above Bolton who were fourth from bottom. After being runners-up the previous season, that was obviously far from satisfactory for everyone concerned. Things weren't running smoothly behind the scenes at this time. I wasn't keen on Buckingham's tendency to have us in for morning and afternoon training sessions. It wasn't a popular move among the rest of the squad either and a number of players went to see Eric Taylor to make the point that we were being overtrained, making us tired before games.

People talk about teams facing hectic fixture schedules nowadays, but it's nothing like we had to contend with back then. For example, that April we played six games in ten days. Imagine players being asked to play as many games in such a short space of time now! We didn't think there was anything unusual about the fixture schedule because it was what we were used to, so you just got on with it. When we were playing that amount of games, we weren't in full training because it wasn't necessary.

After a 3-2 win over Blackpool, we suffered back-to-back defeats against Manchester City and Nottingham Forest. But we made a strong finish to the season, winning our final four games to finish in sixth place. That included a comprehensive last-day victory over Burnley, who finished runners-up to champions Ipswich. Burnley had lost their title chance when they failed to beat Chelsea two days before coming to Hillsborough. We grabbed the initiative from the start and Colin Dobson scored a hat-trick in a 4-0 win. My old foe Andy Lochhead led the Burnley attack, but he wasn't very effective that day, missing several good chances. I always had a tough time against Lochhead who I rate as probably the hardest centre forward I ever played against. No matter how hard you hit him, he always came back.

As we prepared for the start of the 1962/63 season, David Layne, who was to feature prominently in my life, arrived from Bradford City. He was a Sheffield lad who'd previously played for Rotherham. David was a big guy, but he also had plenty of skill, making him a very effective centre forward. He replaced Keith Ellis whose main asset was his aerial strength.

In our first four games of the season, we were near the bottom of the table after picking up just a couple of points. One of those points came in a midweek 3-3 draw at Leicester. Before the Leicester game, Buckingham had a go at David Layne for wearing rubber studs. David had got some new boots which weren't comfortable, so he switched to a spare pair with 'rubbers' on. Everyone was walking around and you could hear the 'clunk, clunk' sound of conventional studs as the players paced around the dressing room before we were due to go out. But of course David wasn't making a noise because of the rubbers and that didn't go unnoticed.

'Layne,' Buckingham bellowed.

'Yes, what's the matter boss?' David replied.

'What have you got on?'

'I've got rubbers. I couldn't put my others on boss because they hurt me too much, so I put these on.

'It's going to get wet out there tonight with the dew and everything else. Be it on your head…'

We came back from 2-0 down to earn a point with Layne, making only his second appearance for Wednesday, putting two goals past Gordon Banks. He scored one from outside the area and then intercepted a back pass from Len Chalmers before rounding Banks and slipping the ball into the net. At the end of the game, as David took his boots off in the dressing room, Buckingham walked past. David couldn't resist making a comment after what had been said before kick-off. 'These boots aren't bad boss, are they?' he quipped. Buckingham cursed him and walked away. David particularly enjoyed getting the better of Banks that night because he'd been at school with Gordon and played in the same Sheffield Boys' side as him. They meet up now to play golf and I'm told those two goals still get a mention!

Buckingham wasn't the type of manager who ruled by fear, throwing teacups around in the dressing room, but I recall seeing him losing his rag at half-time in a game against Burnley. Colin Dobson, who was only a young lad at the time, had struggled in the first half against the Burnley full-back John Angus. Buckingham told Dobson that he had been unhappy with his work rate. 'Colin, John Angus hasn't fucking broken sweat against you,' he said.

'Well boss, I haven't either,' Dobson replied innocently.

It was the wrong thing to say and Buckingham hit the roof, taking off his trademark trilby hat and throwing it on to the dressing room floor in disgust.

David Layne continued to do well in front of goal, scoring twice in a 5-0 win over Birmingham and also netting in the games against Fulham and Leyton Orient. It was such a good side that we were creating a lot of chances for the front players. Before we secured a point in a 2-2 draw at Sheffield United, Layne was interviewed by a *Daily Express* journalist. David had bought a café in Hillsborough and he agreed to do an interview there. When David was asked what he thought about United's Joe Shaw, he gave his honest opinion. 'I don't know why centre forwards seem to get bottled up by him because he's not big enough to start with,' he said. 'If he comes up with me for headers, he hasn't got a chance.' Joe used to play off the centre forward and sweep up behind, very effectively I might add, but David was making an observation. The following day, David was dismayed to read a story in the *Daily Express*, quoting him as saying that he was going to destroy Sheffield United! He had not said that at all, but his quotes had been twisted. The journalist involved never got another story off David because that was the last time he agreed to do an interview with him.

We were on a £4 win bonus at that time, but Mr Whitlam was still paying us a £10 bonus, which made quite a difference. It was assumed that the money came out of Mr Whitlam's own pocket, which he may have won on the fixed odds. But we didn't know that for sure because it could have actually come out of the club's coffers.

With players knowing that their time would be up when they were thirty-five or so, a few of them had different businesses while they were still playing. David Layne had his café, while Tony Kay was a partner in a fencing business. John Fantham had a hairdressers shop and Alan Finney had a paper shop. David's café was a popular place because in those days people would go to a café at night to drink coffee. We would go straight from training to the café for half an hour or so before going home.

Wednesday organised a friendly against the Brazilian side Santos in October 1962. They were the reigning World Club Champions and it was their first visit to England. A certain player called Pelé was in the Santos side and his presence at Hillsborough captured the imagination of the Wednesday supporters who were desperate to see him in action. Pelé was twenty-two and had already won more than thirty caps for Brazil.

After Santos took a 2-0 lead, Billy Griffin and David Layne scored to make it 2-2, but they went on to beat us 4-2. It might have been different had David not been forced to go off after going over on his ankle because he was our penalty-taker and we were awarded a penalty which was missed by Colin Dobson. David had also been causing all sorts of problems for the Brazilian defenders and they were frightened to death of him. It was like when Nat Lofthouse caused problems for continental sides. They didn't know how to handle the big lads.

Merchandise relating to Pelé was highly sought after, as illustrated in the programme editorial:

> In Rio de Janeiro, three years ago, the police arrested a man who was doing very well in selling the shirt of Pelé, worn at the World Cup Final of 1958. The fellow was stopped after having sold forty-two shirts!

I decided to secure my own Pelé memento, only mine would be genuine. It was in my mind all the game to get his shirt. I didn't tell anybody, but I was determined to get it. There weren't many foreign teams coming over to England to play in those days, so shirt swapping wasn't a common occurrence and nobody thought about getting Pelé's shirt. I decided to follow Pelé towards the end of the game. I wasn't supposed to be marking him, but I made sure I was only a few yards away from him wherever he went in the closing minutes. As soon as the final whistle went, I took my shirt off and gave it to Pelé in exchange for his. My teammates followed suit and swapped their shirts with opposition players. Just think, Pelé has probably got a Peter Swan shirt hanging up on a wall in his home in Brazil!

The attendance figure for the Santos match was officially around 49,900, but Hillsborough held 65,000 at that time and you couldn't get a seat anywhere in the ground. There was no way they would have got another 15,000 in, so somebody must have wiped up a few quid that day!

There was controversy in our home game against Aston Villa when David Layne was sent off after clashing with a Scot called James McEwan. Several fans ran onto the pitch in protest and cushions were thrown from the stand. David had taken a few whacks from McEwan at set pieces and they were both lining up for a corner which was being taken by Alan Finney. David realised that McEwan was preparing to clatter into him again, so he sidestepped him and struck out, knocking his teeth out in the process! McEwan protested loudly to the referee, but the officials had not seen a thing. After consulting with his linesmen, the referee had a word with David. 'My linesmen didn't see anything and neither did I, so I'm letting it go,' he told him.

The referee restarted the game with a bounce-up and it appeared that David had got away with it. But the Villa captain, Vic Crowe, noticed blood on David's hand from where he had hit McEwan and pointed it out to the referee. 'Look at his hand, look at his hand,' said Crowe. The referee asked David to let him have a look at his hand and he saw the cut. Pointing to the wound, he asked David, 'How have you done that?'

'I did it in the first half when I fell on the perimeter and scraped my hand,' David replied.

'I don't think you did, off you go.'

David later had to attend a disciplinary hearing, during which the referee made a false claim about what he had seen. Addressing the panel, he said, 'I saw the player Layne strike the opposing player McEwan. I attended to the injured player and after I'd seen to him, I sent Layne off.'

'That is a downright lie,' David responded.

But before he could say anything else, one of the members of the panel ordered him to keep quiet. 'Layne, you can't speak at this hearing,' he was told.

Nobody questioned the referee as to why he restarted the game with a bounce-up, a decision which gave the clear indication that he had not seen anything. David was handed a seven-day suspension and fined £100, which was paid by the club. The lads also had a whip-round for David and he ended up with more money at the end of the week than he usually got!

When David was suspended, Keith Ellis came into the side for his first appearance of the season. Keith was a big, bustling centre forward with a lot of skill, but David was a better all-round player. He could lay the ball off, hold it up and finish well. David was given the nickname 'Red Barrel' because he drank the beer of that name. If we went to pubs where they served Red Barrel, that was what he would ask for. We all enjoyed a good drink after a match, but nobody went over the top during the week in terms of drinking. David later became known as 'Bronco' after Bronco Layne who was a cowboy character on television. David hated the nickname – and still does – so we called him it even more just to wind him up!

As we prepared for the game at Ipswich on 1 December 1962, I couldn't have imagined that I was about to get involved in something which would wreck my career and turn my life upside down.

10

The Biggest Sports Scandal
of the Century

A training ground chat I had with David Layne and Tony Kay was the prelude to what became known as 'The Biggest Sports Scandal of the Century'.

There were a lot of betting scandals in the lower divisions in those days and everyone in the game knew about what was going on. A former player called Jimmy Gauld, who was at the centre of it all, had played with David Layne at Swindon. They met up one night when David decided to go with another Wednesday player, Eddie Holliday, to see Mansfield play West Ham in a midweek Cup replay. David and Eddie were unable to get into the stand at Field Mill because it was full, so they used their players' passes to get in the players' entrance. They were told by stewards to go up the tunnel and get in where they could.

As fate would have it, they bumped into Gauld in the tunnel. The only reason Gauld was down there was because he had suffered a broken leg and it was in a pot, preventing him from sitting in the stand. David and Eddie had a chat with Gauld and they got together again for a drink at the end of the game. That was when the subject of betting came up, with Gauld telling them that players were earning bundles of cash.

The following morning, David came up to me in training and said, 'I was with Jimmy Gauld last night, Swanny. They want another team to get a treble up on the fixed odds. We're at Ipswich that day, what do you think? How do we usually go on there?'

'Well,' I said, 'Ipswich are a bogey side for us and we never beat them. We've got nowt to come.'

It was true because Ipswich were flying at the time and we had a very poor record against them. We just never seemed to be able to beat them. Leicester were another side we struggled against at that time. It's one of those quirks in football; you get teams who always seem to do well against a particular side. We were also in the middle of a terrible run, having gone eight games without a win, so I felt it was likely we would lose at Portman Road.

As David and I continued to discuss our prospects, Tony Kay joined in the conversation and he agreed that it was unlikely we'd win. It was at that point that we decided to place a bet. We knew that two other games – Lincoln City *v.* Brentford and York City *v.* Oldham Athletic – were being fixed to result in home wins, and we thought it would be sensible to put our money on a victory for Ipswich. An Ipswich win was the likely outcome and we were all clear on the fact that we would definitely not throw the match. 'Well, we've got nothing to lose,' I said.

David, Tony and myself were close. We spent a lot of time together socially, going out partying and meeting up with our wives on a Saturday night. We trusted each other and it was just the three of us who placed the bet, no other Wednesday player was involved. When the scandal broke, there was some speculation suggesting that Ron Springett may have been involved. But no, Ron played no part in it. The odds on an Ipswich victory were 2/1 and I gave David fifty pounds. He and Tony were putting the same amount on. That would give us a hundred pounds each, plus our stake money back, which was quite a lot of money back then. We thought it would be a nice bonus and besides, in our eyes, we weren't really doing anything wrong. Okay, so it was against the rules, but we felt that we were going to lose anyway. After David collected the money, he took it to Jimmy Gauld to place the bet. It was later revealed in court that Gauld placed the bets on 29 November 1962 – two days before the Ipswich game – in the name of 'Mr Parry'.

We were travelling to London to spend the night there before heading to Ipswich the following day, so I met up with the rest of the players at Sheffield Midland Station on the Friday morning. A journalist called Tony Hardisty, from the *Sheffield Star,* was travelling with us for the first time. I could sense that he felt like an outsider, so I put him at ease by having a chat with him before introducing him to all the players. The relationship between players and journalists in those days was very different to what it is now. Journalists from the local newspapers would travel with us to games and if we went out for a drink, they'd come with us.

On the journey down to London, it was the usual sort of trip to an away game with players having a laugh and a joke. Some played cards while others just chatted. After booking into the hotel and having our evening meal, we relaxed by going to a cinema in the West End to watch *Mutiny on the Bounty.* On Saturday morning, a coach picked us up from the hotel to take us to the train station. We arrived in Ipswich and had lunch at a hotel five minutes from the ground. There was nothing different about my preparation for the game. It was the same as it had always been and I felt no more nerves than usual in the build-up to kick-off.

Ipswich took an early lead through Ray Crawford who turned the ball home after it had struck a post. Crawford added a second goal on thirty-five minutes. There was nothing out of the ordinary about either of the goals. I had done nothing to help Crawford score, but I can honestly say that I still don't know even now what I'd have done if we'd been winning. As a defender, I was obviously in a position where I could have scored an own goal, which is the easiest thing to do. You can make it look as though you are trying to make a clearance and then spin the ball into the back of the net. Alternatively, I could have pulled someone down for a penalty, which would also have been very easy.

To this day, I don't know whether I'd have done anything to change the course of the game if we'd been ahead. As it was, nothing the three of us did in the game affected the outcome. We just approached the game as normal, played our usual way and got beat. That was illustrated by the fact that Tony Kay won the Man of the Match award in *The People* and David Layne also got the highest rating in the forward line.

It was about three weeks before we received our winnings from the bet. It was later claimed in court that I had bet on numerous lower league games I knew to be 'bent', but that was totally untrue. Admittedly, I would often bet on the fixed odds, as a lot of players did in those days, even though it was against the rules. I never won anything, though. As for betting on Wednesday to lose, the Ipswich game was just a one-off. Whether it would have led to something else, I honestly don't know.

A week after the Ipswich match, our poor form resulted in the attendance dropping to less than 16,000 for the visit of Liverpool, which we lost 2-0. The alarming dip in form resulted in various discussions being held behind the scenes. When Vic Buckingham was quizzed about his plans to try to improve the situation, he told journalists that we were in a 'very rough stream' and said that 'airy-fairy plans' weren't the answer. He added that the only way out was through hard work.

1 Lining up in the Armthorpe Secondary Modern School football team. I'm second from the right on the back row.

2 The Army football team in Germany. I'm at the front on the far right and my best mate Eddie Colman is on the far left. Others pictured who became professional footballers include Jimmy Armfield, Maurice Setters, Alan Hodgkinson, Graham Shaw, Trevor Smith and Stan Anderson.

3 Having a stroll at Skegness with my wife Norma and eldest son Carl.

4 Good arrer! At a
fundraising darts night.

5 A family outing,
complete with
neighbours' children.

6 Sons Carl and Gary,
along with the latest
addition to the Swan
family, Peter junior.

Above: 7 Taking my place in the Sheffield Wednesday line-up before a game at home to Arsenal during the 1956/57 season. I'm third from the left on the back row.

Below left: 8 The programme for Sheffield Wednesday's FA Cup tie at Manchester United on 19 February 1958 – United's first game after the Munich air disaster. I was a regular in the Wednesday side from that day on.

Below right: 9 Programme for Sheffield Wednesday's final home game of the 1958/59 season, celebrating our promotion to the First Division.

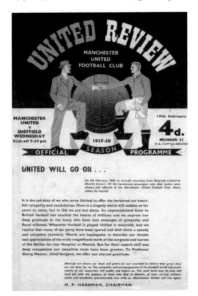

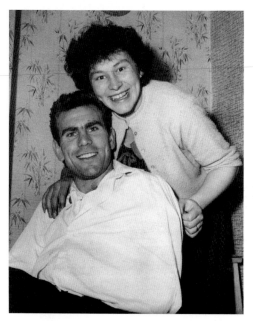

Top: 10 Sharing a joke in training. From left to right: Norman Curtis, Ron Staniforth, Tony Kay, Don Gibson, me, Derek Wilkinson, Peter Johnson, Jimmy McAnearney, Alan Finney, Redfern Froggatt, Roy Shiner, Tom Eggleston and Harry Catterick.

Above left: 11 My arm is in a sling after suffering a dislocated shoulder in a coach crash following the Boxing Day game at Arsenal in 1960.

Above right: 12 Keeping my eye on the ball in training.

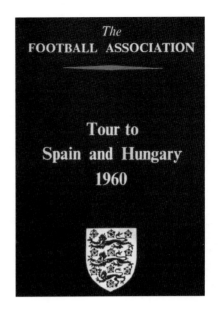

Top left: 13 Itinerary for my England debut match at Wembley.

Top right: 14 Itinerary for the tour of Spain and Hungary. I was glad to be given the opportunity to go away on tour after a difficult debut.

Above: 15 Playing head tennis over the garden fence with next-door neighbour Don Megson. Norma chats to Don's wife Yvonne while a young Gary Megson looks on.

Above: 16 Sheffield Wednesday squad from the 1960/61 season. I'm fourth from the left on the back row. We finished runners-up to double-winners Tottenham that season.

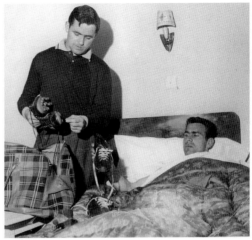

Above left: 19 A member of England's 1962 World Cup squad in Chile. It proved to be a terrible experience.

Above right: 20 In my sickbed in Chile with Sheffield United goalkeeper Alan Hodgkinson looking after me.

Right: 21 Posing for the cameras!

Opposite below left:
17 Programme from Sheffield Wednesday's Fairs Cup quarter-final first leg against Barcelona in February 1962.

Opposite below right:
18 Programme for the Football League *v.* Italian League match at Old Trafford in November 1961. It was the fifth of my six appearances for the Football League side.

22 Training on my own in the pub yard shortly before my ban from playing was lifted.

23 Celebrating with David Layne after being told the *sine die* ban had been lifted.

24 Sheffield Wednesday manager Derek Dooley welcomes David Layne and I back to Hillsborough in 1972.

Right: 25 Pre-season
training before the
1972/73 campaign as
I prepare to make my
comeback.

Below: 26 Sheffield
Wednesday squad for
the 1972/73 season. I'm
second from the left on
the back row.

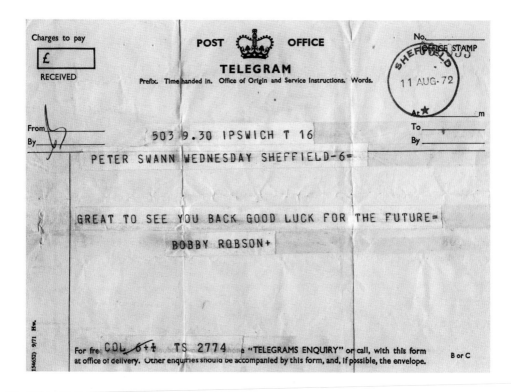

Above: 27 A telegram from my old England teammate Bobby Robson, welcoming me back after eight years out.

Left: 28 The programme for my comeback match against Fulham on the opening day of the 1972/73 season.

Opposite below: 30 Still wearing my short shorts at Bury.

Above: 29 With my new Bury teammates, second from the right on the third row, at the start of the 1973/74 season. Manager Allan Brown is seated in the middle of the second row and the man who replaced him, Bobby Smith, is far left on the third row.

31 In the dugout as manager of Matlock Town.

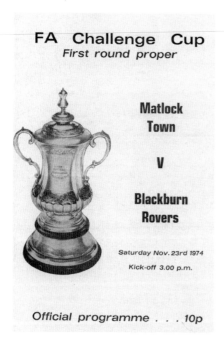

Above left: 32 Programme for Matlock's FA Cup tie against Blackburn in November 1974. Sadly, there was no giant-killing on that occasion.

Above right: 33 Matlock's finest hour! Programme for the memorable FA Trophy final victory over Scarborough at Wembley in April 1975.

34 Back on the Wembley turf after a thirteen-year absence.

35 Nick Fenoughty rounds off the scoring in the 4-0 win over Scarborough.

36 Touring the streets of Matlock, parading the FA Trophy, before a civic reception.

37 Cheers! Pictured after taking over as licensee of The Three Horseshoes in Brimington, Chesterfield.

38 The Three Horseshoes football team. I'm second from left on the back row with three other members of my family. My lads Gary (fifth from the left, back row), Craig (to the right of Gary) and Peter (second from the left, front row) are joined by my brother Terry (second from the right, back row).

39 The Swan brothers. From left to right, back row: Mick, Stan, Terry Bernard, Len and Billy. Front row: Me, Jack and family friend Gary.

40 Admiring the various items of memorabilia which used to be on display at The Mill. They included shirts swapped with Pelé and John Charles.

41 With Norma behind the bar at The Mill.

42 Meeting up again with Sir Bobby Robson when he was in Chesterfield for a book signing in 2005.

We were boosted by the return of Johnny Quinn for the visit of Everton. Quinn, who had been held in the Royal Signals for an extra six months' National Service, sent a telegram to Buckingham to inform him that he was set to return home. David Layne was also back in the side after suspension. Quinn and Layne played key roles, both scoring in a 2-2 draw. On an icy pitch, we outplayed Everton and deserved to win. The game marked Tony Kay's last appearance in a Wednesday shirt as he moved to Goodison Park just days later in a £55,000 transfer, which was a record fee for a half-back. Everton players were among the highest-paid in the country, so Tony would have been given lucrative terms. Kay had won seven England Under-23 caps during his time at Wednesday and later won a full cap. He went to live in the Liverpool area following his transfer to Everton and I more or less lost contact with him.

Following Kay's departure, I was named as the new Wednesday captain. It was a real honour to captain the club and I loved it. There was great pride in running out onto the pitch with the ball under your arm, hearing the roar of the crowd as you emerged from the tunnel. I was actually in dispute with Wednesday over a new contract around that time. My basic wage was £20 a week and with appearance money and bonuses, the figure would go up to about £40, but I wanted more. The year before, my England teammate Johnny Haynes became the first player to earn £100 a week when the maximum wage was abolished, which was big news at the time. I reasoned that as I was also an England player, I deserved to be given a rise. I asked for a basic £40 a week, knowing that other payments would take this up to about £60. The Wednesday board refused to meet my demands, so I decided to hand in a written transfer request. I explained that I wasn't happy with the terms of my new contract and stated that I wanted to be made available for transfer, but the letter was promptly torn up! In an attempt to put the board under pressure to increase their offer, I told them I wouldn't sign the new contract I'd been offered and signed a monthly contract instead.

Given the fact that I was in dispute with the club, I was surprised when Buckingham decided to hand the captain's armband to me. 'Why make me captain when I've put in for a transfer and I'm not satisfied?' I asked him. Buckingham explained that I was the player he wanted to lead the side because he thought I would do a good job, so I agreed to take on the role. When you're in a good side and winning regularly, you have little to do as the captain, so it made little difference to me on the pitch. In all honesty, the responsibility was shared throughout the team, so I felt that we didn't really need a captain. It was more or less just a case of going up to shake hands with the opposition captain and giving a call for the toss of a coin.

It wasn't long before I decided to give up my bid to secure a better deal. The club held my registration and they made it clear they weren't prepared to let me go, so I signed the contract I'd been offered. The clubs had power over the players at that time and basically dictated whether you were staying or going. If a player in the current game wanted an improved deal, they can engineer a move to another club with the help of an agent.

Even though I was not getting paid as much as I thought I was worth, I was happy to put an end to the uncertainty and pledge my future to Wednesday. I was happy at the club and had forged a good relationship with Vic Buckingham. I was impressed with the fact that Buckingham valued and respected my opinions as captain. He would invite me into his office in the build-up to a game and ask me what I thought about the opposition and discuss tactics. That would not have happened with his predecessors, Eric Taylor or Harry Catterick. They simply told you what they wanted and wouldn't ask you to contribute any ideas.

David Layne, Tony Kay and myself naturally kept quiet about the winning bet we had placed. But I did hint at what had happened in a conversation with a national newspaper journalist called Frank Clough at a Christmas party held by David Layne. I got chatting to Clough about what was happening in football at that time. 'Frank, I could tell you something that's happened which would shatter English football,' I said. He asked me to tell him what it was. 'No, I'd never do that,' I replied. That must have got him thinking long and hard. As a journalist, he would have been desperate to find out what I was referring to, but there was no way I was going to give anything away, so we just left it at that. Whether he later put two and two together and worked out what I was talking about, I don't know.

Freak weather conditions at the turn of the year caused havoc with the fixture list. Only three of the thirty-two FA Cup third-round ties due to be played at the beginning of January went ahead, with our game at Shrewsbury among the casualties. It was one of the worst winters on record and we went nearly two months without playing, from 12 January to 4 March. With snow and ice on the ground making it impossible to train outside, we were forced to go indoors. We didn't have a proper gym at Hillsborough, so arrangements were made for us to use the facilities at Sheffield University. We played five-a-side games and head tennis, but it was no substitute for playing in competitive matches. After going weeks without playing, there was a lot of frustration among the players, with a lot more fights in training than at any other time. Players would go in for challenges that little bit harder than usual and sometimes things boiled over with punches being thrown, but things were soon forgotten and there were never any lasting feuds.

With such an horrendous fixture backlog, the season had to be extended by a month and we were faced with playing twice a week for the rest of the campaign. In some ways it actually made things easier for us because the amount of matches we were playing meant there was less training. The break seemed to do us some good because we went on a winning run when things got back to normal. A 3-0 win at West Brom in mid-January ended a sequence of 12 games without a victory and saw us move up five places in the table. It was nearly two months before we played again, but victories over Nottingham Forest, Manchester City, Blackpool and Wolves made it five wins in a row.

As we prepared for the trip to Birmingham at the end of March, Gerry Young had a match of his own to think about as he was getting married on the morning of the game. After being out of the side and thinking that he wouldn't be involved in the first team, he'd made the arrangements for the wedding, only to receive a recall a fortnight before the Birmingham game! In order to take his place in the start-ing line-up at St Andrews, Gerry had to leave the church as soon as the marriage ceremony finished and make an eighty-mile dash from Sheffield to Birmingham. Gerry played as an inside forward when he first got into the side, but he was moved back to replace Tony Kay and later won an England cap as a wing half. He had broken his nose and it was very flat, so we used to say that he'd been window shopping too much! Gerry was a smashing lad; he was very quiet and kept himself to himself. He stayed in digs after coming down to Sheffield as a young lad and I regularly invited him back for meals because we had a house near the ground soon after getting married.

When Tottenham came to Hillsborough, it was perhaps inevitable that I would be compared to Maurice Norman who had taken my place in the England team. I was pleased with my form at that time and there were calls for me to be recalled to the national side. I was up against Tottenham's centre forward Les Allen and hardly gave him a chance as we won 3-1.

David Layne scored twice in a 4-0 win over Blackburn to take his tally for the season to 26 and many felt he deserved a call-up to the England squad. We experienced a mixed set of results in April, winning 4 and losing 4. We faced Liverpool at Anfield at the end of the month, just two days after they had suffered an FA Cup semi-final defeat against Leicester at Hillsborough. I kept Ian St John in check and Tom McAnearney had a superb game against Jimmy Melia.

Games were coming thick and fast due to the backlog and our victory over Bolton in early May made it four wins in the space of just eight days. Our penultimate game of the season was a derby clash with Sheffield United at Hillsborough. United included a young Mick Jones, who went on to play for England, in their forward line. After going down to ten men early in the game when Joe Shaw went off injured, United took the lead. But we came back to win 3-1 following two goals from David Layne and another from Tom McAnearney. We ended the campaign with a 3-2 defeat at Arsenal and finished in sixth place, which was a good achievement after such a poor run from the end of September until January.

Mark Pearson, who was a Sheffield lad, joined Wednesday from Manchester United early in the 1963/64 season. He had made his debut for United against Wednesday in the first game after the Munich air disaster, but failed to hold down a first-team place during his time at Old Trafford. He had the nickname 'Pancho' because of his Mexican-style sideburns, but he was quoted in a newspaper article saying that he wanted to lose the Pancho image. As soon as he walked into the dressing room for the first time at Hillsborough, we all said, 'Pancho, how are you going on?' He didn't have a chance of losing the name because everyone knew him as Pancho. Pearson was a quiet type of lad who settled in really well and I regularly used to go out drinking with him. It's a pity he wasn't a bit taller and a bit faster because he had a lot of skill.

Pearson scored twice in our Fairs Cup second-round first-leg tie against Cologne in Germany. We were never in it during the first half and found ourselves 3-0 down at half-time. But we fought back through Pearson's goals to cut Cologne's advantage to a single goal. Remarkably, both goals were direct from corners. It was great going on trips abroad because we had such a laugh. There were all sorts of things we would do to lighten the mood. One thing I used to do was to put a pair of women's knickers in my roommate's suitcase before we set off back to England. The player would then be faced with an irate wife when she unpacked the suitcase at home, asking where the offending item had come from. 'I've not seen them before, Swanny will have put them there,' the player would protest.

Another high-scoring game followed when we drew 4-4 at Stoke, with Layne and Pearson scoring two apiece. We found ourselves 4-1 down with eighteen minutes to go before hitting back to level at 4-4 after scoring three goals in six minutes. Vic Buckingham played hell with me because John Ritchie, the man I was marking, scored a hat-trick. I thought I'd had a good game because Ritchie, who joined Wednesday a few years later, had only had three kicks or headers that day. The problem was that they all went in. I didn't think any of the three goals Ritchie scored were down to me because he got them when I wasn't there!

We went out of the Fairs Cup after losing 2-1 against Cologne in the return leg. I was going up for corners, trying to help force a goal, but we got caught on the break and lost 5-3 on aggregate. I could hardly be considered a threat at set pieces after failing to score a goal for Wednesday. David Layne would lose patience when another of my attempts to score came to nothing. He'd say, 'What the hell are you doing here? Get the fuck off back where you belong, we don't need you up here. That's what I'm here for, to score goals.'

Colin Dobson was brilliant when we beat Wolves 5-0. He had great ball control and trickery, but he was a shy lad who lacked aggression. If he'd been more aggressive, he'd have been a world beater because he could beat six or seven men with his skill. A full-back could frighten him and if I'd have been playing against Colin, just one good, hard tackle would have put him out of the game. Saying something to him would have had the same effect. Colin played for the England Under-23s, but never won a full cap and that was probably down to the fact that he didn't push himself forward. He preferred to stay in the background and it showed in his play. Eddie Holliday, who also played on the wing, was so fast he could catch pigeons. The problem was that he would sometimes forget to take the ball with him and he didn't have a lot of heart. A full-back would frighten him and if he received one kick, he wouldn't go past the player again.

Considering they had been a bogey side for us, we were delighted to record a 4-1 win at Ipswich. David Layne, who scored a hat-trick at Portman Road, also got a goal as we beat Sheffield United 3-0 at Bramall Lane in the following game. That saw us move up to fourth in the table in the middle of January, but there was disharmony behind the scenes. Trainer Jack Mansell did all the coaching and Vic Buckingham would pick the team. 'Go out and entertain the public,' he'd say to us before we went out. Mansell and Buckingham then fell out over something and they weren't really on speaking terms towards the end of their time together at the club. While Buckingham was giving a team talk, Mansell would be shaking his head. 'What a load of crap he's talking,' he'd mutter under his breath.

Wednesday went through a spell when Mark Pearson, Eddie Holliday and Alan Finney all got in trouble for drink-driving. The members of the board were not happy with the fact that several first-team players had appeared in court and some of them blamed Buckingham for the disciplinary problems. It was unfair to blame him in my opinion because it wasn't his fault, but Buckingham had his contract terminated soon afterwards. Buckingham was unlucky really because he got sacked after we finished sixth in the old First Division three years in a row. What would Wednesday give now to finish that high?

More than a year had passed since the Ipswich game, so it wasn't at the forefront of my mind. There was nothing to suggest that the topic would resurface, but shortly before news of the scandal broke, my mum gave me what proved to be a prophetic warning. I used to visit my parents as often as I could. If I got complimentary tickets for a game, I'd go over to Doncaster with them, so I usually went on a Friday night, about once a fortnight. I was sat with my mum on one occasion when she suddenly announced that she was worried about me. 'You're going to be in some trouble,' she said. 'I don't know what it is, but you're going to be in very big trouble, so just be careful.' I didn't take the warning seriously, partly because I never really understood her interest in spiritual matters. My attitude to it was, 'Well, if trouble comes, trouble comes.' I never gave another thought to what my mum had said until the scandal broke and then her words came back to me.

On what seemed like a normal midweek day, I was getting ready to go to Hillsborough for training. I was doing something in the house when two cars pulled up outside. A total of four people got out of the cars and they looked like CID officers. I said to Norma, 'There's somebody coming, it looks like the police, something must have happened.' They walked up the drive and knocked at the door. I made sure our dog, who was barking and going crazy, was safely out of the way before I opened the door. I then came face to face with a fella who introduced himself as Mike Gabbert from *The People*. He said, 'We've just been to David

Layne and he's owned up to fixing a game at Ipswich. He says you had a part in it.'

'If you think that, go and see my manager,' I replied. They were the only words I spoke to him because I then closed the door. The fella with Gabbert, a journalist I later learned was Peter Campling, appeared to be holding a book, which I was told could have concealed a tape recorder. I knew straight away of course that I was going to be in trouble. I had not helped fix a game, but I'd had a bet on my team to lose and that was against the rules. My first instinct was to speak to David Layne. The other player involved, Tony Kay, was no longer at Wednesday, so it wasn't as easy to get hold of him.

The journalists stayed in their car outside my house for quite a while, so I waited for them to go before getting in my car and driving over to see David. He confirmed that he'd seen Mike Gabbert and Peter Campling from *The People*. David had his café in Hillsborough at that time and he'd been interviewed by them there. Prior to that, Jimmy Gauld had paid an unexpected visit to David's café. Saying that he wanted to have a chat with David in private, Gauld invited him to go outside and sit in his car. The subject of the Ipswich game cropped up and, unbeknown to David, Gauld had a tape recorder hidden underneath one of the car seats, which he used to record their conversation. The recording was later played in court and I understand that our case was the first one in British legal history where the use of taped evidence was allowed. When Gabbert and Campling appeared at David's café, they told him they had reason to believe he had been involved in match-fixing. 'I hope you've got some kind of proof,' David replied.

'Read that,' instructed Gabbert as he produced a transcript of David's conversation with Gauld.

David looked at the document which detailed everything he had discussed with Gauld in the car. Gauld had told *The People* that there were some high-profile players involved in match-fixing and obviously wanted to make a fast buck. In order to do that, he had to get the evidence which would incriminate us.

Faced with the damning evidence in front of him, David was told by Gabbert and Campling that they were going to help him as much as they could. They assured him that he would not be in any trouble if he co-operated with them. 'We're not after you at all,' they said. 'We're after the bookmakers and the people who've made bundles of money out of it.'

David was a gullible lad in his younger days and he fell for it, opening up to them and it all came out. If he hadn't done that, it's likely that nothing would have happened. David was also told that if he signed a legal document, stating that the bet was a one-off incident, it would help all concerned. He agreed and was taken to a Sheffield solicitor who was known by one of the journalists. The document was duly typed out and David signed it, without receiving advice from his own solicitor, giving *The People* an affidavit which was produced in court. When David met the solicitor at a party a year or so later, the solicitor apologised for his conduct. 'I'm terribly sorry about what happened,' he said. 'If I'd have known what was going to happen, I would have advised you not to sign it.'

'As a solicitor, you should have advised that I had another solicitor there, acting on my behalf, before I signed it,' David replied.

When David told me what he had done, admitting what had happened, I wasn't happy, so things got a bit heated between us and we fell out. 'I'll deny everything,' I told him.

Things happened quickly because just a few days after David had spoken to Gabbert and Campling, the story that was to change my life appeared in *The People*. The front page headline was sensational, to say the least: 'THE BIGGEST SPORTS SCANDAL OF THE CENTURY'. I'd never met Jimmy Gauld – the first time I saw him was in court – and yet, according to *The People*, I was supposed to have had meetings with him and David. Gabbert wrote that I'd openly confessed and signed a document stating that I'd been bribed. That was not true, because all I had told Gabbert was to go and see my manager and it was the last I saw or heard of him before the scandal broke. *The People* also claimed that David had admitted to taking a bribe.

David decided that he had to see Wednesday general manager Eric Taylor on the Saturday night after being contacted by a journalist who told him that the story was in all the 'papers in Manchester. David phoned Taylor at his home and asked if he could see him urgently. Not realising the seriousness of the situation, Taylor was initially unwilling to meet him. 'I'm sorry David, I've got some visitors, so it'll have to wait,' he said.

But David was insistent: 'Look Mr Taylor, it's a matter of life or death, it can't be shelved at all. I've got to see you.'

Taylor relented and agreed to see David, inviting him to come to his house in the Fulwood area of Sheffield. David drove over there straight away and spoke to Taylor in his lounge. David struggled for a few moments to find the right words before Taylor interrupted him. 'I'm way ahead of you,' he said. 'I know what's happened because since you phoned me, my phone has never stopped ringing.'

'Well, I just thought that I'd got to tell you straight that it was my fault. It wasn't the fault of Peter Swan or Tony Kay,' said David.

'Right, come and see me on Monday morning.'

David then met up with me because we had arranged to go out for a drink at a pub in Derbyshire. While we were out, a message was relayed to David from journalist

John Sadler of *The Sun*, advising him not to return home because the press were out in force, waiting for him. At that time, David lived at the café he owned in Hillsborough and he had to go back to take the babysitter home. When David returned home, there were dozens of reporters, photographers and cameramen there. Reporters were climbing up to bang on the windows, hoping to secure an interview with him. The babysitter, who was an elderly woman, was frightened to death because she did not have a clue what was going on.

Eric Taylor phoned me on the Sunday morning and said that he wanted to see me in his office with David the following morning. I was frightened to death as I prepared to come face to face with Taylor for the first time since the scandal had broken. I had a lot of respect for him and felt I had let him down. When David and I reported to Taylor's office, he was angry and upset, but all we could do was to explain to him that Ipswich were a bogey side and that we'd not fixed the match. We were due to face Tottenham at Hillsborough that night. The game should have been played on the Saturday, but it was put back forty-eight hours because there were a number of players from the two clubs involved in the England *v.* Scotland international that weekend. Taylor asked us both if we wanted to play against Tottenham. We were both adamant that we did want to. 'Well, you're going to get some stick, you know that,' said Taylor.

'If I miss a goal, I get some stick anyway,' David replied, 'so what difference does it make? You know if I score one, there will be 50,000 cheering, so it won't make any difference.'

Taylor gave it some thought and agreed. 'Right, you're playing,' he said.

Our hopes of turning out were ruined, however, when the FA contacted Wednesday officials later in the day to inform them that we were barred from playing with immediate effect.

Taylor informed of us the development. 'There's nothing I can do,' he explained. 'I've got to suspend you, but you're suspended on full pay. Until it's sorted out, I don't want you near the ground until I call on you to bring you back.'

There was of course intense media coverage of the story, so on behalf of the Wednesday board, Taylor read out the following statement:

> The directors have been shocked by the allegations of bribery implicating certain members of the club's playing staff which were published in a Sunday newspaper. Such serious charges will form the subject of an immediate investigation by Sheffield Wednesday and the club will give all the help that is within its power to assist any other inquiries which may be instituted.
>
> In view of such pending inquiries the directors cannot make further comment on the subject beyond emphasising that the first intimation of any such allegation of bribery came to the notice of the club in the publication of the newspaper article today. The members of the playing staff who were named in the newspaper article have been released from their club duties pending the result of the inquiries into the charges.

Not surprisingly, there was intense media interest in the story and the following day's front page headline in the *Sheffield Star* read: 'SOCCER SENSATION – PROBE OPENS'. The editorial said:

> Police inquiries were opening at Sheffield today into allegations made in a Sunday newspaper against soccer players. Sheffield Wednesday last night suspended two of their players – centre forward David Layne and centre half Peter Swan – while they make their own investigation.

Mr Dennis Follows, secretary of the Football Association, said of the allegations, 'We shall have to take notice of this, following our normal procedure in handing over any evidence we might get to the police.

Mr Joe Richards, president of the Football League, said he presumed that the FA and the League would be considering the matter and 'perhaps following the normal procedure and appointing a commission'. He added: 'It is a serious report. Obviously, I don't know how far it is true, but it cannot be ignored.'

Mr Cliff Lloyd, secretary of the Professional Footballers' Association, said, 'Naturally we are very disturbed at what we have read but at the moment I can make no further comment.'

The *Sheffield Star* revealed that the South Yorkshire Police Superintendent, William Bowler, had taken personal charge of the investigation into the allegations. Bowler was quoted as saying, 'Sheffield police are studying newspaper reports about the allegations. But as yet no fixed line of enquiry has been decided on.'

The South Yorkshire Police Chief Constable, Edward Barker, added, 'Whenever there is a suggestion that a criminal offence may have been committed we look into it. We have read the press reports and we are looking into the case although I can't say where our inquiries will take us.'

Wednesday chairman Dr Andrew Stephen and vice-chairman Harold Jessop had apparently been travelling back together on a train from Scotland when they read the story in *The People*. Attempting to obtain Dr Stephen's reaction, a journalist from the *Sheffield Star* visited his home, only to find he was out on his calls. But his wife was quoted as saying:

> To say my husband is upset is putting it mildly. He is absolutely stunned and shocked, floored beyond belief. People who know my husband know that this kind of thing is the one thing that would upset him more than anything else. He – and the club – have a reputation throughout soccer as straight-shooters.

After being suspended, I was faced with the fact that I wouldn't be able to play and it was difficult to take in. *Sheffield Star* journalist Ross Jenkinson came to my house, but I closed the door on him. He persisted, however, in trying to secure my reaction to the suspension. 'I'm your friend Peter,' he shouted through the letterbox, 'I won't write anything you don't want me to write.' I relented, invited him in and told him the whole story, detailing what I knew and what we'd done. Jenkinson was the only journalist I spoke to and he wrote a big piece, based on what I had said. 'It is a terrible blow not being able to go to the ground and club I love so much,' I said, continuing:

> I am not going away, because whatever there is to be faced I shall face here in the city that has been so good to me. My heart will be out there with the lads against Tottenham tonight. I can't even begin to tell you how upset I am. My wife is, too. It's terrible, just terrible.

Vic Mobley, who was a twenty-year-old centre half, was handed his home debut as my replacement. It must have been a daunting prospect for a lad of his age to make his first appearance at Hillsborough, especially given the circumstances. But he did well and didn't let the occasion get to him. Mobley was built like a bodybuilder; it was all natural as he didn't do any weights. Personally, I didn't rate him as a player and I wasn't all that keen on him.

Eric Taylor made an emotional speech to the supporters at half-time, urging them to 'bear with the club in this most tragic affair'. Taylor, who was greatly respected in the game, was deeply affected by the scandal. 'These allegations are horrifying in the extreme,' he said. 'Nothing like this has happened to me in all my years in football. It is the biggest blow this great club has ever had to take.'

My relationship with David Layne was strained at this point. I blamed him for opening up to the *The People* and felt very hostile towards him. I had no interest in speaking to him and 'sent him to Coventry'. We didn't utter a word to each other, or even look at each other, when we were in training. I was so bitter that if we had spoken, it would no doubt have resulted in a slanging match and probably have got out of hand. I therefore took the view that it was best to ignore him completely. Things remained difficult until a tragedy later brought us back together.

David and I were in limbo during the period leading up to the court case. We were allowed to go back training until the case came up, but we had to train with the young lads. Alan Brown, who had been at the club as a trainer when I was a part-timer, had just returned as Vic Buckingham's replacement and he wouldn't allow us to train with the first team. It was frustrating because we were training as normal, but couldn't play. It all seemed so pointless, but we carried on as best we could in the circumstances. During one training session, Brown played the first team against the young lads and I was put with the young lads. The first team were hammering us by about seven or eight goals and I was upset because they were taking the piss out of the young lads. I didn't think that would be any good for the youngsters, knocking their confidence, so I made my feelings clear to Brown. 'Well, if that's teaching young lads how to play football...' I said. 'You've got first-team play-ers taking the piss out of fifteen-year-olds.' I felt that the manager shouldn't have treated the youngsters like that, so I walked off the field in disgust while the match was still being played.

After training all week and then having no match to look forward to, my frustration boiled over during that incident on the training pitch. It was something I shouldn't have done, of course, but the pressure must have got to me with the court case looming. I returned to Hillsborough and Brown, who'd turned religious in the years after his first spell with Wednesday, got me in his office. I was sat down waiting for him and when he walked in, he said, Don't sit there, stand up. You walked off that training pitch, which was an insult to me and your teammates.'

Brown then started preaching to me, telling me about the error of my ways. 'Do you go to church?' he asked.

'No, I'm Church of England, but I don't go to church,' I replied.

'Well, you should go home and start praying to God for forgiveness for what you have done. God will then look after you. Trust in the Lord and you won't have a problem.'

I came close to bursting out laughing before he told me to go. I wasn't interested in what Brown had to say because I wasn't religious, but he clearly had strong belief in his faith and thought that I would benefit from his advice. Brown, who had spells as manager of Burnley and Sunderland between his two stints at Hillsborough, was a very hard man who ruled with a rod of iron. He stood for no messing about and you knew where you stood with him because he was like a very strict headmaster. It was fair to say that Brown had changed a lot when he came back to Hillsborough. He had apparently been a bit of a lad when he was younger and there was a tale going round that he'd confessed all his wrongdoings to his wife after he'd turned to religion. How true that was, I don't know.

As the case drew closer, David and I had to stop training after being instructed by Wednesday officials to stay away from the ground and stop mixing with the rest of the players. The players were even ordered to stop visiting our homes. It was difficult for the club to prevent Don Megson from seeing me because he lived in the semi next door! There were two others, Robin Hardy and Eddie Holliday, who took no notice of the ban and they used to come to see me straight after training. There were no problems with any of the players because they all gave David and me their support. I couldn't understand why they were told they had to keep away from us, unless the club thought there were others involved in the scandal.

I missed the camaraderie with the lads in training because we always used to have a laugh, winding each other up and playing practical jokes. I desperately wanted to resume training and continue with my career, but after being found guilty of conspiracy to defraud, it would be eight years before I went on a training ground again.

11

Banned *Sine Die*

I may have regained my freedom after leaving prison, but my life remained in limbo. There was still the matter of my future as a professional footballer to be resolved, although I was in no doubt that I faced a lengthy ban from the game.

When I was sentenced to prison along with Tony Kay and David Layne, FIFA president Sir Stanley Rous said, 'One can only hope that the strong action that has been taken will act as a deterrent to others.' It was clear, however, that our punishment would not end there. All three of us were notified of a meeting with the FA at Lancaster Gate, but I told my wife Norma that I would refuse to go. 'It would be just a waste of money going to London because I know what they're going to say,' I said. I knew that a ban would be the outcome, whether I attended the meeting or not. Tony and David decided to go down to London.

It had been speculated in the build-up to the meeting that we faced lifetime bans from the game. I didn't know we'd been banned until I saw the news on television. I sat watching the box at home and learned that we had been banned *sine die*. The Latin phrase means 'with no appointed date', so it was for an indefinite period.

Written confirmation of the ban subsequently later arrived via Eric Taylor at Sheffield Wednesday. I will be for-ever grateful for the support I received from Wednesday at that time. I'd been suspended on full pay up until the court case and Wednesday also paid my solicitor's fees, which was brilliant of them. I don't know how much the bill came to, but it must have been a substantial sum.

The suspension prevented me from being involved in football at any level. As it was enforced by FIFA, it was a worldwide ban.

I felt, as many did, that we had been treated very harshly. We were sent to prison, we got fined and we were banned for life from football, so we got three punishments. They crucified us in every way to make an example of us. My solicitor wanted to fight the ban on my behalf. 'Peter, they cannot stop you from playing football,' he said. 'I want to take it further and fight it for you. How much money have you got?' Apart from the fact that I had used up all my savings, I was fed up with the whole situation because it had been going on for so long. I decided against pursuing it and informed my solicitor of my decision. 'It's dragged on and on and I've had enough,' I said. 'I'm going to get a job and get on with my life.'

My solicitor was insistent and tried to persuade me to change my mind. 'They cannot do it to you,' he said. 'They cannot stop you earning a living.' But I had made up my mind that I would go out and get a job, which meant start-ing again from scratch.

My relationship with David Layne remained strained until he was involved in a serious car crash a few months after coming out of prison, which sadly resulted in his wife Caroline being killed. It must have been an awful time for him, with all the uncertainty surrounding his future, then losing his wife in such tragic circumstances. David was recovering from his injuries in hospital and I couldn't help thinking about what he must have been going through. I told my wife Norma, 'He must be in a shocking state. I've got to go and see him.' So I went to visit him in hospital and he was delighted to see me. We settled our differences straight away and we've been friends ever since.

Because the scandal was such a big story, I was inundated with phone calls from national newspaper journalists who wanted to interview me. But I was so bitter about what had happened that I ended up insulting them. Following the lies that had been printed in *The People*, a newspaper reporter was the last person I wanted to speak to. Ironically, *The People* had been the paper I read every Sunday prior to the scandal, but I've never read it since. I won't have it on principle and neither will any of my family. My parents in particular were very bitter and they cancelled delivery of the paper straight away. They had been loyal readers of *The People* all their lives, but they wouldn't read it after what had been printed about me.

One journalist who did manage to speak to me before I slammed the phone down was from a Sunday tabloid who wanted to write what he called a 'wine, women and song' story. It would have been full of scandal, involving drinking and womanising – all of it made up – and I just had to put my name to it. In return I would have been paid £10,000, which was a lot of money in those days. I was tempted by the offer and spoke to my wife about it. 'Let me do it,' I said. But I couldn't persuade Norma to go along with the idea. 'No,' she insisted, 'we've got kids growing up and they'll get teased at school.' So that was that, I had to turn down ten grand. It was a great temptation because it was easy money and if it hadn't been for the kids, I would have done it.

When I'd got done, I was on a £40-a-week basic wage, plus bonuses. You'd get a crowd bonus, a bonus for keeping in the top six and there was also so much per point. The highest wage I came out with was £105, which was a lot of money then. I was getting money for playing for England as well, which worked out at £50 per game plus expenses. All things considered, I was doing well, so it was difficult to adjust after being forced to pack in football.

As soon as I learned that I was banned *sine die*, I discussed the situation at length with Norma. 'What am I going to do?' I said. 'I've got to work because I've got a mortgage to pay, what am I going to do for a job?' The only job I'd done before becoming a footballer was going down the pit as a sixteen-year-old kid. I didn't know what I was going to do until a friend of mine, who worked at Fletchers Bakery in Sheffield, phoned to offer me a job. 'Swanny, I've got a job for you if you want it,' he said. 'We haven't got anyone covering the area where you live on the retail bread side. I'd like you to go round all the householders. What do you think?'

'Yeah, brilliant,' I replied, 'I'll have a go at it.'

I established a round in Stannington, where I lived, going round in a van, selling bread and cakes. I'd drop orders off to regular customers and others would buy from the van. I enjoyed the work because it was in my own area and I was going to people I knew. I had only been working for Fletchers for about four months when I was offered a car sales job.

An old assistant secretary at Sheffield Wednesday called Ted Gibson had left Hillsborough to go into the motor trade. He phoned me one day and said, 'Swanny, would you like a job?'

'Doing what?' I replied.

'I'm sales manager at Shukers Car Sales and we could do with another salesman.'

'But I know nothing about cars,' I admitted.

'Don't worry, I'll teach you everything. Just listen to me, pick up some of the sales talk and you won't go wrong. You don't need to know anything about cars to sell them.'

So I finished at Fletchers and went to work at Shukers, selling new and second-hand cars. Morris Minors were very popular at the time and we sold a lot of those. If I remember right, a brand new Morris Minor estate car sold for about £600. I was put with Ted who taught me the sales patter and, despite my lack of knowledge, I started selling a lot of cars and soon became the top salesman! A lot of it was down to the fact that Sheffielders were coming to me because they knew who I was. Lots of people came just to talk to me about football and you could tell the ones who weren't interested in buying a car. They would pretend to be looking for a car, but in reality all they wanted to do was talk to me about Sheffield Wednesday or football in general.

I enjoyed the job because it allowed me to meet all sorts of people. There were some real characters. I remember on one occasion falling for a trick when I took someone for a test drive. A guy had been looking at a car and asked if he could take it for a drive. 'I want a good ride in it to make my mind up,' he said before we set off.

'Yeah, that's alright,' I replied.

I got in the passenger seat and we drove off from the sales pitch, which was in the centre of Sheffield. After driving several miles to the Manor Top area of Sheffield, he stopped the car, got out and said, 'No, I don't want it.' He then went into a nearby house and I realised he'd just tricked me into letting him drive himself home! I didn't fall for that one again.

Every salesman on a car pitch knows which cars are good and which ones are bad. If I knew someone had been saving up to put a deposit on a car and was buying it on hire purchase, I used to put them off a car which I thought was a bit dodgy. But I'd also get the type who thought they knew everything, saying things like, 'Oh, you can't tell me anything about a car.' In those circumstances, I would let them buy a car I knew to be a bad buy.

I was on £12 a week, plus commission on every car I sold, which was five per cent of the profit made on the car. In those days, there was a lot of profit made on the sale of a car and I presume it is the same nowadays. They could go and buy a car at auction for £20 and sell it for £120. There would also be a bonus for being the best salesman. Ted did most of the actual selling, but he'd put it down to me, even when I wasn't there and it meant I was coming out with a good wage. I also had a company car, which was a nice perk.

I'd sometimes go and watch matches at Hillsborough with a lad called Jimmy Drabble, but I'd only go to the night games, standing right at the back of the Spion Kop. I wouldn't go on a Saturday because I didn't want people to recognise me. In truth, it was terrible watching the games, but then I never was a good watcher even when I was playing because I wanted to be out there. Even now, when I'm watching football on television, I know where the ball should be.

There was a brief hope of resurrecting my playing career in 1967 when a Canadian club called Toronto Falcons wanted to sign me, David Layne and Tony Kay. David got in touch and informed me that Toronto's representative had approached him. I then got a phone call from the representative who explained that we'd be part-time players and that jobs had been lined up for us. He added that we would also be sorted out with apartments and cars, so it appeared to be a decent package. I told the Toronto representative I was interested, but said that I'd have to discuss it with my family. The chance to move to Canada sounded exciting and we would also be given a chance to play football, which was the best part about it. All three of us agreed to the deal and signed contracts, but just as we were about to get plane tickets to fly over, the representative came back to us a couple of weeks later and was apologetic. 'We're sorry, but we can't sign you,' he said. 'We're trying to get in FIFA and they've banned you, so that's it.' If they signed three players who had been banned by FIFA, they would not get in, so they had to scrap plans to sign us.

Disappointed at missing out on a chance to pick up the pieces of my football career, I continued to earn a living outside of the game. After spending two or three years at Shukers, I bought a shop in Doncaster. Harry Davidson, who was related to me through marriage, had a shop in the Rossington area and when we met one weekend, he asked me what I was doing.

'I'm just selling cars,' I told him.

'Well, next door to me there's a shop which is coming up for sale,' he said. 'They sell hardware and cycles and it's a good shop. I'd have a crack at it if I were you. Are you interested?'

The shop was located in the market place and it appealed to me, so I went with Norma to see it. Norma didn't want to go initially, but she eventually changed her mind and we decided to buy it. There was a flat above the shop, so we sold our house and moved there. Things went well for a while, but a supermarket opened up at the other side of the market place and they sold the hardware I was selling, taking away a lot of my trade. I considered the possibility of going all towards cycles because I wasn't doing bad with them. I sold second-hand cycles and also had an agency for Raleigh, but the sales weren't enough to make a good living.

When I was considering what to do next, my former Wednesday teammate Keith Ellis invited Norma and me over to his pub in Maltby one night. He asked me to give him a hand because he was short of staff, so I went behind the bar with him and enjoyed it so much that Keith asked me if I wanted to do some bar work. I accepted the offer and started travelling two nights a week from Rossington to Maltby to work behind the bar before we eventually put in for a pub.

We got our first pub with Stones' Brewery – The Travellers at Attercliffe in Sheffield – in 1968. It was at a time when Attercliffe was swinging because people used to come to the area to do their shopping and trade was good. But then they started pulling the houses down and rehousing people and the area went in two minutes. The brewery kept me in The Travellers, hoping that people would still keep coming in because I was there, but it didn't work, so we got out of there.

I got in touch with Mansfield Brewery who gave me a pub in Chesterfield straight away. I phoned them and had just one meeting when they offered me The St Helens. It was a rough pub, but it was brilliant. I've not had too much trouble in the pubs that I've had, but I had to sort out a problem there before it got out of hand. There had been a spot of bother in the tap room and when I went in to see what was wrong, one of the regulars, a big lad called Malc, made a threatening remark to me. When I went back behind the bar, I said to my missus, 'I've got to go and sort it out.' She tried to talk me out of it, but I knew that I had no option. 'If I don't go now, that tap room will rule this pub because they know I'm a weak man,' I explained to Norma. I opened the tap room door and gestured over to Malc. 'Come on Malc, outside,' I said. We stepped outside and as he came towards me, I hit him, catching him with a good 'un which knocked him out. It was a good job I did because he was a big fella and I don't know what he would have done to me if I hadn't put him down. They had to take him home in a car.

I'm not a fighting man. Alright, I can stick up for myself, but I've certainly never gone looking for a fight. I knew it had to be done though and it worked because word soon got round and the regulars at the pub, who were supposed to be tough fighting men, were as quiet as mice after that! 'That Swanny can put 'em down,' they'd say. By the time we moved to our next pub a few miles away – The Three Horseshoes in Brimington – word had reached there that I was a hard man after sorting out The St Helens. Consequently, the tap room at The Three Horseshoes, which had a reputation for being rough, was quiet and we didn't have any trouble.

12

Comeback After Eight Years Out

When we moved back to Sheffield to take over The Travellers, I started a pub team and played in it. We were playing quite regularly, but they were only friendly games because we weren't in a league.

I also played in some charity games with David Layne who had put a side together at his pub in Rotherham. But then a journalist on a national newspaper got wind of the fact that David and I were both playing. The journalist phoned David and told him that he was going to run the story. David said, 'Why on earth are you getting at us? Why don't you go over to the other side of the Pennines and get hold of Tony Kay because he's playing all over the place for a Showbiz XI. Why don't you get on to him? Leave us alone because we're trying to earn a few quid for charity.'

I then received a phone call from someone at the Sheffield & Hallamshire FA. He said, 'Peter, I hear you're playing football again, how are you going?' I explained that we'd just started a team at the pub and I was enjoying it.

'Well you can't play,' he said.

'Wait a minute, these are friendly games,' I protested. 'Most of them are for charity.'

'You still can't play.'

I couldn't believe what he was saying. 'You must be joking,' I said.

'No, the FA law says you cannot play.'

I was warned that if I played again, they would fine the club secretary and ban the team from playing. They stopped me from playing in the friendly games, but I did play in the games they didn't know about. If someone wanted me to play in a charity game, I'd go and play in it. I used to get round the ban by playing under another name. I would more or less play every week, often turning out for Johnny Quinn's All-Stars, which was a team of retired players who raised money for charity. We went round Yorkshire, helping a lot of people. It seemed ridiculous to me that they were trying to stop David Layne and I playing, but the rules stated that we couldn't play on any ground which came under the jurisdiction of the FA. That meant we couldn't even walk on school playing fields, banning me from even watching my own lads. But of course that didn't stop me. People knew who I was, but they didn't do anything about it because they knew it was such a daft ban.

I enjoyed playing and it helped me keep fit. As an ex-pro, I got quite a bit of stick from opposition players. There'd be a centre forward who'd have a crack at me just to be able to say he'd had a go at Peter Swan, but I just used to laugh it off. I'd sometimes get a bit of abuse from the crowd, especially if we played on a Sunday afternoon, after the pubs had come out. You'd get a few ex-pros in the pub leagues and you got a lot of players who'd nearly made it. There were also ones who were going to make it. I found it easy because they were only amateur players and I'd played professionally, so I was thinking perhaps two yards ahead of them.

I trained on my own and kept myself in good condition because I always had the hope that the ban would be lifted.

I fancied getting back into football and thought that if I did get back I'd be halfway there in terms of fitness. I did a lot of running, going out in the morning and doing a mixture of jogging and sprinting. Some players drink too much and let themselves go when they finish playing. But the pub trade has never been a problem for me as far as the drink is concerned because I've always been in control of myself. I like a drink, the same as anybody else, but I was never a big drinker. I might have a glass of wine with a meal, but otherwise it's rare that I have a drink before 8.00 p.m.

I used to do some ball work in the back yard of my pub, where nobody could see me. I had a wall about eight or nine feet tall and the yard was quite big, so I could kick the ball at the wall and test my control. I also trained at Chesterfield Rugby Club as it was near to my pub in the town. I just did the fitness work there because I didn't like the actual contact involved in playing rugby. I had a go at playing once, but it was too rough for me, so I did all the running with them when they trained. If they played a game, I stepped aside.

Matt Busby was one of the people backing the call for our ban to be lifted. Eric Taylor was also fighting on our behalf, but Busby was the main figure pressing for our return. It was not until some years later that we were told just how much work Busby had done for us. My good friend Jimmy Greaves also wrote about me in his column in *The Sun,* saying that we had served our time and deserved to be allowed back. Jimmy's a great bloke and I appreciated his support.

One high-profile figure who was against the idea of us making a return was Brian Clough. He was quoted in one of the national newspapers saying that we shouldn't be allowed back and that upset me a lot at the time. But I put my feelings to one side a few years later when Clough brought his Nottingham Forest side to play against one of the non-League clubs I managed. To arrange the match,

I spoke to Clough's assistant, Peter Taylor, who asked for half the gate money. He told me he wanted it in cash, which would be shared out among the players, but I doubt whether the players saw any of the money. When I welcomed the Forest players and officials to the club, Clough never even looked at me, and after he had turned his back on me, I made no attempt to talk to him.

I remained hopeful that our ban would be lifted. Joe Ashton, a Labour MP who supported Sheffield Wednesday, came along to talk to me at my pub and described the ban as a 'very harsh punishment'. Joe also said that preventing us from appealing against the ban was against the principles of British justice. When Ashton first got into parliament towards the end of 1968, he vowed to take up our case. After being prevented from raising the subject in the House of Commons, he was later advised by a journalist on *The Times* called Robin Oakley to write to the Sports Minister, Dennis Howells. Howells replied, informing Ashton that it was not within his power to do anything, but he did promise to pass the letter on to the FA who agreed to review the case. I later learned that Ashton received a lot of flak from the business community who were involved with Sheffield Wednesday. Businessmen who were on the board at Hillsborough, or held shares in the club, were not happy with the fact that Ashton was helping to get the ban overturned. Wednesday have always had a proud standing in the game and they no doubt felt that the case tarnished the reputation of the club.

The newspapers speculated that the ban was about to be lifted and they reported that I could go and sign for any club. Non-League clubs like Matlock, Alfreton and Gainsborough came in for me, but I had hopes of playing League football again. Just before the ban was lifted, I organised a charity night at my pub where we played cards, dominoes and darts. Chesterfield FC sent a team which included their manager, Jimmy McGuigan. Jimmy came up to me at one point during the night and we talked about football. He brought up the subject of my possible comeback: 'It looks as though your ban is going to be lifted, what are you planning to do?'

'Sheffield Wednesday have still got my registration, so I'm hoping to play for them again,' I replied.

'Well, before you go back to Wednesday, come down to Saltergate and I'll prove to you that you've been out of the game too long and convince you that you can't come back.'

'We'll have to wait and see,' I said before bringing our chat to an abrupt end.

What he said really annoyed me because I'd been building myself up to return to playing and he was trying to shatter my dreams. People were generally sympathetic to my cause and wishing me well, but McGuigan tried to take away any hope I had of returning to the game.

When the FA reviewed the case, their lawyers agreed that it was against the principles of British justice and we were notified that the ban had been lifted at a hearing we were told to attend at the Grand Hotel in Leicester.

Eric Taylor, who was still the secretary and general manager at Hillsborough, phoned me to discuss the situation. 'You're still a Sheffield Wednesday player and from what I've seen of you, I think we can do something because you don't look much different to when you went.'

That was great to hear. 'Oh, brilliant,' I said. 'Whether I'll be able to come back or not I don't know, but I'd like to give it a try.'

I went to see Eric the following day and he was emphatic in his desire to take me back to the club. 'Your registration is stopping here,' he said. 'We want to have a look at you.' I was delighted to hear that because it was what I had been hoping for. David Layne was also invited to rejoin

Wednesday and he too accepted the opportunity with open arms. It was obvious that it would not be as easy for David to make a comeback as it would be for me because he had let himself go, putting on a lot of weight. He'd always been heavy when he played before the ban, but of course he was much younger then.

The manager was Derek Dooley, who had been a fearsome centre forward for Wednesday in the 1950s. He was like a big rhino charging through defences and he got goals off every part of his body. Derek's playing career was cruelly ended when he lost a leg after gangrene set in following the fracture of the limb in a game at Preston. When Derek told the Wednesday board that he wanted to take David and myself back to Hillsborough, his plan wasn't met with universal approval. The Wednesday chairman, Dr Andrew Stephen and several directors were far from keen when Dooley put the suggestion to them. We didn't know at the time that there was any opposition to our return, but some people apparently could not forgive us for what we had done. Dooley was not of the same opinion and wanted to give us a second chance. He felt that we had served our time and been punished enough. Arguing our case, he said that if either of us were half as good as we were before the ban, we would do a good job for Wednesday. After listening to Dooley, the directors who opposed our return decided to put their personal feelings aside and support the plan to give us a chance. Dooley later said he felt it was the 'human and proper thing' to allow us to resume our Wednesday careers.

As it was pre-season when we went back, David Layne and I were starting at the same time as the other players following the summer break. I didn't find the training much of a problem because I was near enough at the same fitness level as the others, but it could have been different if I'd gone back halfway through the season. As it was, it came naturally to me and didn't seem such a big step. David did find the training difficult though. He failed to break into Wednesday's first team during his second spell at the club, but he did make a few appearances on loan at Hereford.

I initially signed for a month on £20 a week. At the end of the month, when I had proved my fitness, I was handed a contract until the following summer and my wage was increased to £50 a week. There were players at the club I'd never heard of, including skipper David Clements, but they all gave me a good reception.

Dooley had strengthened the squad over the summer, bringing in several players including Scottish winger Willie Henderson, so hopes were high going into the new season. Dooley was quoted in the *Sheffield Star* as saying, 'The Second Division will throw up about twelve of twenty-two clubs as promotion candidates – and I am confident Wednesday can make a big impact.' In the same article, Dooley warned David Layne and me that we could expect no favours. He said:

> They have been training hard and will have to produce as much effort as everyone else and be subject to the same discipline. It is entirely up to them whether they play soccer for Wednesday this season. They will be considered with the rest and merit alone will decide whether they are chosen.

I proved my fitness in training and was rewarded with a place in a seventeen-man squad for a pre-season trip to Scotland, but David Layne was ruled out due to a thigh injury. We began the trip with a game against East Fife and I was named as a substitute. I made my first appearance in a Wednesday shirt following an eight-year absence when I came on as a replacement for John Holsgrove half an hour from the end. My timing was a little out, to say the least, after being out of the professional game for so long. That was noted in the following day's match report in the

Sheffield Morning Telegraph. It read, 'His timing was rusty at the start, but by the end he was moving impressively and had cause for satisfaction.' After conceding an early goal, we came back to win 3-1 with Willie Henderson laying on two goals for Brian Joicey and Mick Prendergast scoring the other. Henderson had been signed on a free transfer from Glasgow Rangers. Derek Dooley was happy with my performance. He told the *Sheffield Morning Telegraph,* 'Peter did very well once he had adjusted himself to the pace. It's always difficult to come on as a substitute, let alone after such a long time.'

I was left out for the following game against St Johnstone, which we again won 3-1, but I made my first full appearance in the final game of the tour against Dunfermline. We won 4-2 and things had gone well because I was beginning to develop a good understanding with my central defensive partner, John Holsgrove.

I really enjoyed featuring in the games in Scotland and my contribution went some way towards convincing Dooley that I was worth a place in the side at the start of the season. In the build up to the opening-day game at home to Fulham, Derek took me to one side for a word. 'Peter, you're in on Saturday,' he said.

I'm a bit sentimental, so the emotion got to me and I'm not ashamed to say that I wept when I heard the news. After regaining my composure, I wanted to assure Derek that I would justify his decision. 'I'll not let you down,' I told him.

News of my inclusion in the starting line-up was made public a couple of days before the game. *Sheffield Star* journalist Tony Pritchett wrote:

Peter Swan has made it! The former Wednesday and England centre half goes straight into the Owls team on Saturday for the new season's first game against Fulham. Swan ended one of the great storybook comebacks in soccer this afternoon when his name was included in the teamsheet, pinned up in the dressing room at Hillsborough by team manager Derek Dooley.

Dooley said that I had been rewarded after proving my fitness and my ability in pre-season. He commented:

> He did great things in Scotland and this, after his remarkable enthusiasm in training, convinces me that he is ready for League football again. Saturday's match will be a great day for Peter. It will not only be a test of his ability; it will be a test of his emotions. I am sure he has the character to rise above it all. I hope this is the start of a new life for him.

I spoke to *Sheffield Morning Telegraph* journalist Martin Leach on the eve of the game, telling him how thrilled I was to be included. 'The funny thing is, two years ago I seemed to have been out of the game 100 years, but the way I feel today I was never out at all,' I said.

I received many telegrams and cards before the game, wishing me well, which was tremendous. Among the telegrams I received was one from my former England teammate Bobby Robson. It read, 'Great to see you back – good luck for the future.' Bobby's a nice man and it was good of him to do that. A few years later, when he was manager of Ipswich, he visited my pub with his players on their way to an away game.

Derek Dooley was very supportive and he said some nice words in the match-day programme. He said:

> I am sure that you would like to join me in congratulating Peter Swan on his return to football. Peter has shown enormous personal courage in fighting to attain the degree of fitness necessary to regain his place in our first team.

He has shown great dedication and has been determined to prove a point – that point being of course, that he retained his flair for the game and is fit enough to compete. Peter has worked tremendously hard in pre-season training and he got himself well involved in our practice matches and on our Scottish tour in which he played his part in helping us to a hat-trick of victories. He is over the first hurdle. There is, however, a long way to go but Peter has done a fine job and the staff here at Hillsborough wish him every success.

I approached the game by telling myself that I was starting at the same level as the rest of the players who had been on a summer break. I was given the captaincy to mark the occasion and they let me take the ball out. I went down the tunnel just ahead of the other players and ran out on to the pitch, thinking they were still there, but they had stayed behind, leaving me to run out on my own. The reception I received was unbelievable and I could have cried because it was such an emotional occasion for me. From the centre circle, I raised my arm to salute all four corners of the ground.

When the game got underway, the fans cheered my every move. Even when I went to take a throw-in, I was applauded for that! It was brilliant. I was involved in the opening goal, launching the ball upfield to Brian Joicey who played it on for Mick Prendergast to fire home from the edge of the box. Fulham, who included Alan Mullery in their side, were rarely in the game and we went on to win 3-0. A number of journalists were waiting to interview me after the game and I told them how tired I felt. 'I was always tired after a match when I played before,' I said. 'But who cares. I loved every minute of it.'

Derek Dooley was quoted as saying, 'Peter has proved what I have said all along – that he can do a good job for us. He certainly did it today.'

Reporting on the match in the *Sheffield Star*, Tony Pritchett wrote:

A crowd almost double last season's first-day turn-out welcomed Peter Swan on his return. Swan completed his marvellous comeback story with a near-flawless performance. Maybe it wasn't one of the Second Division's classic show-downs. But on a day of stripes, Swan and sunshine, who can complain about a 3-0 win?

Derek Dooley was brilliant and I thought the players should have kicked their own grannies for him because of what he was doing for them. He had the former West Ham player, John Sissons, who for me was the best winger in the land at that time. But Derek couldn't get him to go down the wing because he wanted to tip-tap the ball in midfield. If Harry Catterick had been the manager, he'd have made him do it. Derek was a good manager, but for me he wasn't hard enough with the players.

I developed a good understanding with John Holsgrove. John would go for the balls when they were played over the top and I'd cover at the back. If he missed them, I picked them up. It worked well until a game against Nottingham Forest when these high balls were coming over and John wasn't going, so I was caught in two minds. At the last minute, I'd be going and making a mess of it because of the confusion. I said, 'John, you're not going for them, what's the problem? I don't know what I'm doing.'

'You play your fucking game and I'll play mine,' he replied.

Why he said that, I don't know, but I could have hit him. In fact, if it hadn't have been for the fact that I'd just come back, I think I would have smacked him. Derek Dooley couldn't see the problem and I made only two more appearances before being dropped. Derek explained he was resting me and said I would still be paid first-team money, including win bonuses. I told Derek that I wanted to play if he felt I was the man for the job, but I didn't play for Wednesday again. I had made 13 appearances in my second spell at Wednesday, taking my total for the club to just over 300.

The game had changed a lot and it seemed to me that everybody wanted to play in midfield. In all honesty, I had struggled because the pace of the game had changed that much during my absence. I'd been out too long and it was too much for me. I was too old and I was never really going to come back as a Second Division player. I think things would have come right somewhere near the end of the season, but it wasn't to be.

I was satisfied because I'd proved to myself that I could get back and that was a big achievement after being out for so long. If I hadn't made a comeback, I'd have always been left wondering, so I'm glad that I did. I also proved the doubters wrong; people like Jimmy McGuigan who had confidently predicted I wouldn't be able to return. I felt like phoning McGuigan after my comeback game against Fulham and having a go at him.

Derek Dooley was prepared to give me a contract for a second year and let me play in the reserves, helping to bring on some of the younger players. But after waiting so long to play in the professional game again, I wanted first-team football. After I was informed that I would be allowed to move on if another club came in for me, Dooley said that Chesterfield and Bury were interested in signing me. I was also told by someone that Doncaster were interested. Having supported them as a kid, I would have loved to have joined Doncaster. But I heard nothing from them, unfortunately.

A move to Chesterfield interested me more than Bury. They were in the Third Division for a start, a division higher than Bury. I was also living in Chesterfield, with a pub in the town, so there would be no problems over travelling. I had talks with the Chesterfield manager, Joe Shaw, who I'd admired so much as a player for Sheffield United. Joe said that he wanted me to help bring his youngsters on in the reserves. He added that he didn't want me for the first team, but I think he knew that I'd get in the side.

The talks went well and at the end of our discussion it appeared certain that I would be joining Chesterfield. 'I'll get the contract drawn up and then give you a ring to arrange the signing,' said Joe. But my hopes of signing for the club were dashed when Joe asked the Chesterfield board to give him the go-ahead to complete the transfer. As promised, Joe phoned me a few days after our meeting and it soon became clear there was a problem. 'I'm sorry Peter, I can't sign you,' he said, explaining that the directors wouldn't sanction the transfer because I had a pub too near the ground. Whatever difference that made, I don't know, but they were apparently adamant and told Joe that he couldn't sign me.

I was disappointed because signing for Chesterfield would have been ideal for me and my family. I expressed my disappointment to Joe. 'I'm hoping one day to become a manager and I think that if I wanted to sign a player, I'd sign him, regardless of what the directors said,' I told him. 'You're doing a job and that's what you're paid to do.'

But I knew that whatever I said to Joe would make no difference. With Chesterfield out of the running for my signature, I had talks with Bury and joined them instead.

13

Promotion with Bury

Signing for Bury saw me drop down to the Fourth Division, which suited me down to the ground after struggling with the pace of the game in the Second Division.

They were looking to improve on their mid-table finish the previous season and manager Allan Brown felt my experience would be a useful addition to the side. I enjoyed playing under him because he knew how to handle players. He was happy to let me travel from Chesterfield to Bury twice a week, recognising that travel takes more out of you than training. 'All I want you to do Peter is come over here two days a week and then we'll see you on the Saturday,' he said. 'You don't need all the travelling, so it would be better for you to spend two days with us and spend the rest of the week training with Sheffield Wednesday.' So I did that and the arrangement worked well.

I was handed the captaincy of the side and made my debut on the opening day of the season at home to Torquay. I got my Bury career off to a flying start, scoring after only three minutes – my first ever League goal. I'd gone all through my career at Sheffield Wednesday without scoring a goal in League football and yet managed to find the back of the net just a few minutes into my debut for Bury. It was a header from a corner and I went up to the goalkeeper as he was picking the ball out of the back of the net, patted him on the back and said, 'Don't worry son, the best can't get them!' It was great to finally break my duck.

The reason why I hadn't scored for Wednesday was because in those days, centre halves didn't tend to go up for corners and free-kicks like they do now. You'd sometimes go up for a corner if a late goal was needed, but I was never really encouraged to go forward. Every time I did go up, it was usually a bad corner. It was either one played to the near post or a low one. I managed to score in both nets when I was playing for the English League against the Scottish League at Ibrox. I was very frustrated after scoring an own goal, so I went up for a corner near the end of the game and managed to head an equaliser.

Our first away game was at Workington and I roomed with goalkeeper John Forrest. In the hotel the night before the game, I said to John that we should go and look to see if any of the lads had left their room unlocked. The plan was that we would go in and rearrange the furniture or do something else for a laugh. But unbeknown to us, Derek Spence and Steve Hoolican had similar ideas. They sneaked into our room while John and I were out and we came back to find they had squeezed toothpaste into a bottle of wine I had taken along, cut the bristles off our tooth brushes and hung up our suits and other clothing outside on the balcony! Players always used to get up to tricks to relieve the boredom on away trips. A common stunt was to find someone's toothpaste and squeeze it all out, leaving them with an empty tube.

I felt brilliant at Bury and we had a good young side. There were a lot of youngsters who hadn't made it with bigger clubs. Derek Spence, who was a young lad then, was a forward with a lot of potential and he went on to play for Northern Ireland. David Holt was my central defensive partner. He was a good, young player and we had a good understanding. If I went up for the ball, 'Holty' would come round me to provide cover and vice versa. He was a nice lad and I was sad to hear that he had died at the age of fifty-two after suffering a heart attack. We had an outside left called George Hamstead and John Murray, an inside forward. They were both very good players.

I got into the habit of having a drink of wine or a neat whisky before going out on to the pitch. I think it was physio Bob Little who advised me to have a shot of whisky to warm myself up. There had always been a bottle of whisky in the Sheffield Wednesday dressing room for players to take a drink from before a game, but I didn't do that when I was a younger player. It was only when I got older and wasn't as fit that I felt I needed it as a tonic and I had a drink before every game during my time at Bury. It gave me a lift, especially on a cold day.

I had to laugh when the lads set me up before a game at Lincoln. Knowing that I had served part of my prison sentence in Lincoln Prison, they clearly thought it was a great opportunity for a prank when we played at Sincil Bank. I was out on the pitch, warming up for the game, when the PA announcer said, 'This is for Peter Swan, from the inmates at Lincoln Prison' and then played the Elvis song 'Jailhouse Rock'! I looked over at my teammates who were in hysterics. Laughing, I mouthed at them, 'You bastards!' I thought it was hilarious and it was typical of the type of thing that went on at a football club.

I sometimes used to have the referee on when they came in to inspect my boots before a game. I'd be stood there, facing the wall, with my legs apart, just wearing a jockstrap, along with my socks and boots. Referring to my time in prison, I'd quip to the referee, 'I've been in this situation before.' Some didn't crack their face, but others would have a laugh. If I mistimed a challenge, I'd look at the ref and say, 'I've not got my timing back ref, I've been out of the game for nine years!' You had to know which referees you could say that to.

I had a great rapport with the Bury fans and they would chant my name. When I went up for a corner, as we were waiting for the ball to be retrieved, I'd go round the back of the goal and pump my fist, urging the fans to get behind us.

I used to get some stick from opposition fans over the match-fixing case. I remember one game in particular when we played in front of a small crowd and a bloke shouted something at me when I went up for a corner. Because of the small size of the crowd, I could pick him out, so I shouted back, 'I'm laughing all the way to the bank.' I shouldn't have reacted and I was angry with myself for doing so, but it's annoying when someone has a go at you.

I used to look at the crowd a lot and laugh at them when they were shouting things at me, but fans can go too far sometimes and I can understand it when players react in certain circumstances. For example, when supporters start shouting things about a player's family. That's supposedly what happened to Eric Cantona when he jumped into the crowd at Crystal Palace and aimed a kung fu kick at someone who'd been insulting him. I can understand why Cantona lashed out and I didn't blame him one bit because I think I'd have done the same.

The arrangement over travelling to Bury only twice a week was working out very well until Allan Brown left to take charge at Nottingham Forest in December 1973. Bobby Smith, who had been working as a coach under Brown, took over as manager and he wanted me to travel to Bury every day. I didn't need that at my age and I felt it was unnecessary. Bobby was only a young fella, taking the job at the age of twenty-nine, and I suppose he wanted to impose his authority.

We were due to play Mansfield, which was only a short trip from my home in Chesterfield. 'I'll be able to go straight to Mansfield won't I, Bobby?' I asked.

'No,' he replied. 'I want you to come here and travel with the players on the bus.'

That meant travelling from Chesterfield to Bury, to come back to Mansfield. It seemed ridiculous to me and I was tempted to refuse. It was only because I wanted to play that I took notice of him and travelled. Bobby had been a brilliant coach. In fact, you couldn't have got a better coach because he had a great football brain. But as soon as he took over as manager, he seemed to change and I don't think he liked me, to be honest. He certainly didn't do anything to help me.

Smith could have viewed me as a threat because there was a lot of talk about me taking the manager's job before he got it. I fancied the job, but nobody from the club said anything to me. That might have been on Smith's mind because if I was talking to the chairman, Billy Allen, he would make a beeline for us. Mr Allen was a smashing old fella and I enjoyed chatting to him, but Smithy clearly didn't like me talking to him alone. Whether he was worried that I was going to get his job, I don't know.

Before a game at Gillingham, all the talk was about their player Brian Yeo, who was one of the top scorers in the League at the time. As we were lining up, waiting for the kick-off, I decided to try and unsettle him. 'Who's this lad who's scoring all these goals?' I shouted. 'Is it you, Yeo? You'll not get any today, son.' I was right because we won 2-0. If anybody had shouted that at me, it would have built me up. But some players were put down when you had a go at them and you soon knew which ones were like that.

People now can't believe it when you tell them about the sort of fixture schedule we faced, playing three games in four days over Easter. We were at home to Exeter on Good Friday, faced Doncaster the following day and then travelled to Exeter for a game on Easter Monday. The players would be in uproar if you asked them do that now.

I was sent off for the first and only time in my League career in a game at Swansea towards the end of the season. It was a ridiculous decision. As I went for the ball, one of the opposition players came across to challenge and I went into him. It wasn't a deliberate foul, but the referee sent me off. I was furious with the decision and removed my shorts in protest, twirling them round my finger as I walked off! My conduct landed me in trouble with the authorities as I was hit with a fine.

We had had a laugh the night before the Swansea game when some of the lads decided to do a streak. At that time, there was quite a lot of streaking going off throughout the country. We were staying at a hotel on the seafront and there was David Holt and one or two other players who stripped off and shot out of the front door. They were nearly caught by Bobby Smith who came out of the hotel, no doubt to find out what was happening. The lads were alerted to the fact that the manager was on the lookout and they managed to find a suitable hiding place, slipping underneath the protective covering on some rowing boats across the road. They waited until Smith went back inside before dashing back to the hotel.

A young player called John Thomson took my place when I was suspended for the red card offence in the Swansea game and Smith kept faith with him when I was available again. Thomson was a good player who'd come to Bury after being an apprentice at Newcastle, but he lacked the necessary experience and they lost one or two games in my absence. I went to watch them in a game at

Barnsley and had words with Smithy, telling him that he'd be better with me at centre half due to my experience. I won a recall to the side and later learned that the chairman had ordered Smith to play me.

Promotion was sealed after Northampton failed to win a game in midweek and the following Saturday, before our home game against Newport, the players were handed bouquets of flowers to throw to the fans. I decided to go into the crowd and handed out individual flowers to fans.

It had been a good campaign and we were on a high after winning promotion. But given the relationship between myself and Bobby Smith, I suppose it was inevitable that I would leave at the end of the season. I was gearing up for the match when Bobby came up to me just before we were about to run out on to the pitch. 'Swanny, I've got a bit of good news for you,' he said. 'I'm going to give you a monthly contract next season.'

The timing was unbelievable. I thought, 'Well, what a twat'. I looked at him and replied, 'A monthly contract and we've just got fucking promotion? Surely I'm worth a full contract, like I've got now.' I then added, 'Forget it anyway, you've no need to bother because I'm finishing.'

I'd been in the team all year and I felt let down. Alright, I was getting on a bit, but I was still a fit lad and I could have carried on. But it was not to be and that proved to be the end of my League career.

I helped Bury finish in fourth place in the Fourth Division, six points ahead of nearest challengers Northampton. Peterborough were the champions, with Gillingham the runners-up and Colchester in third place. Our total of eighty-one goals was the second highest in the division behind Gillingham.

Overall, it was a very good time for Bury and I'd have loved to have stayed at the club because I enjoyed it that much. But I wasn't signing another monthly contract because I thought I was worth more than that after helping them win promotion. The players were disappointed to see me leave and I hated moving away from there.

Okay, it had been a bit of a culture shock playing in the Fourth Division after being treated like royalty in the First Division. The facilities were very basic and some of the players had to take their kit home to wash it, although I never did. But I loved it at Bury; it was a smashing little club. The people at the club were friendly and the crowd loved me. It also has to be said that the standard of football suited me then. Playing for Sheffield Wednesday in the Second Division had been too much because of being out for so long, but I enjoyed it a lot more at Bury and playing at that level was a doddle. It was that easy that I think I could be playing there now!

It was a pity in many ways that I only lasted a season at Gigg Lane. There's no doubt that the only reason I came away from there was because of the disagreement I had with Bobby Smith. I think if Allan Brown had stayed at Bury, I'd have played on for another season.

At the age of thirty-five, I was hoping that another League club would come along and offer me a contract. Barrow had just come out of the Football League and they offered me the player-manager's job. They were obviously keen to get back into the Football League and they made me an attractive offer. The deal was on better money than I'd been on at Bury and included a house in the area.

After waiting and waiting for a Fourth Division club to come in for me, I was contacted by Matlock Town who were in the Northern Premier League. I spoke to the chairman and four or five committee men and they came to my pub in Chesterfield to offer me the job of player-manager. After going to Matlock to have a look at the ground, terms were quickly agreed and I was ready to begin my managerial career.

14

Wembley Cup Triumph

I started out in management without any formal train-ing for the job. I had started out on a coaching course, studying for my preliminary badge, when I was playing for Sheffield Wednesday. Players were offered the chance to go to Lilleshall to take their badges and I was one of several representatives from Wednesday who attended the course. But I didn't get the chance to finish it because the scandal broke soon afterwards.

I didn't feel, however, that my lack of a qualification put me at a disadvantage. A lot of footballers are thick, but they know the game. Okay, some lads can't put over what they want to say because they're not good communicators. But those who are good communicators don't need coaching badges, in my opinion, because they're natural footballers.

I needed someone to help me on the coaching side, so I contacted a lad called Harry Peck who I had met when I took my first pub. Harry had been out of the game for years after being at Chesterfield as a youngster, but I decided to offer him the trainer's job and it worked out brilliantly. Harry would take the training sessions after discussing things with me. He also watched our future opponents and then compiled reports, telling me how they played and highlighting which particular players to look out for. All the players enjoyed Harry's methods and we had a good, lively dressing room, which is half the battle. When I eventually left Matlock, I tried to get Harry the manager's job, but he wasn't interested.

I contacted my old England teammate Jimmy Armfield, who was manager of Leeds at that time, for some advice and he very kindly invited me to attend training sessions there. I spent a week travelling up to Leeds every day and picked up various tips on coaching from Jimmy and his staff, just watching what they did and listening to what they had to say to the players. Things weren't much different from when I was playing at the top level. They were saying pretty much the same things, but I still wanted to learn what they were doing at Leeds because they were a top side then. There was a lot of sprint work in the gymnasium, improving the speed of the players. They had a different routine outside, with the emphasis again on speed, getting players to compete in races against each other. My short time at Leeds provided me with valuable experience and I was grateful for Jimmy's help. Jimmy did well at Leeds, taking them to the European Cup final, which they lost to Bayern Munich in controversial circumstances. Funnily enough, I hadn't seen Jimmy as being manager material when we were players because I didn't think he would be hard enough. I always look at a manager as someone who had to be hard with players because I was brought up that way with Harry Catterick. I prefer the type of manager who would say, 'Right, you get out there and you do this.' I should imagine Jack Charlton was like that when he was a manager.

Although I joined Matlock as player-manager, I made it clear that I would not carry on playing if a suitable replacement emerged. 'I'll play, but if I can get a centre half who can do a better job than me, I'll finish,' I told the Matlock committee. I felt that my reputation as a former England international helped me when I was playing for Matlock. It was as though the forwards I played against were worried about facing me instead of concentrating on the game. That meant that half the battle was won as soon as I went on the pitch. There were of course some players at that level who would dish it out. You'd always find someone who wanted to have a go. I've even faced players in charity games who wanted to kick me because I was an ex-player. It's amazing when you think you're playing in a game to raise money, but that's what happens. I bet eight out of ten of them will then go to the pub and brag to their mates that they've kicked Peter Swan.

The Northern Premier League was a good standard. I would say that the top six clubs in the Northern Premier in those days could have held their own in the old Fourth Division. Matlock had never been out of the bottom six, so there was plenty of room for improvement. Things started going well pretty quickly and, in December, we set a new Northern Premier League record when we won 10-0 at Lancaster City. It was a record which stood until 2000.

Working with players on a part-time basis wasn't easy because they had to juggle playing with their day jobs. There were always some players who missed training due to work commitments, so you never had a full squad. If players couldn't get time off work to play in a match, we would still pay their wage. You'd sometimes get a player pulling a fast one, saying they were working when they weren't. Non-League players could earn decent money, adding the cash they received for playing football to the salary from their day job. When I went to Matlock, I put all the players on the same wage. I got them all together and told them what I was doing. 'Right, all the lot of you are going to be on £20 a week,' I said. That was a decent wage back then and they all accepted it. It meant there was no falling out between the players, arguing about what different ones were earning. They were also given a bonus of £2 for a win and £1 for a draw.

I got the players thinking professionally. I asked chairman Cliff Britland if I could get the players together for a pre-match meal, just like the professionals have, and he readily agreed. If we were playing at home on a Saturday, we would meet at a hotel in Matlock Bath. I'd get them in at twelve o'clock for a meal of poached eggs, beans on toast, or whatever they wanted. It made the players feel as though they were at a big club and it's amazing what a difference it made to them. Their attitude changed, acting more professionally than they had done previously.

When it came to tactics, I used to like playing the old way with wingers. I went out to watch games and got two good wingers. There was a lad called Colin Oxley on the right and a player called Andy Wilson on the other wing. If the ball was lost on the left wing, the right-winger would come into midfield, so that we'd got the midfield packed. As soon as we retrieved the ball, the winger would go back out wide. It was like playing a 4-2-4 system all the time and with two fast, tricky wingers, it worked out very well. I thought the game plan we adopted was simple, but when I later went to Worksop, I had a player who couldn't do what I was asking him to do. The lad was so fast he could catch pigeons and League clubs were looking at him. But when I tried to get him to move into midfield when we'd lost possession, he just couldn't grasp it.

We had a brilliant midfield player called Brian Stuart, who was being watched by League clubs. And there were the three Fenoughty brothers, Mick, Tom and Nick. Mick went wide when we retrieved the ball and Nick was very clever with the ball. I got him a trial at Burnley, but he wasn't bothered. He was an idle player, which was a shame because if he'd had the right attitude, I think he'd have been a First Division player. Tom, who had played for Sheffield United and Chesterfield, sat in midfield and sprayed the ball about. Keith Stott, who'd also played for Chesterfield, was a great lad and a very good centre half. He was brilliant for me, putting his head in anywhere. Keith was an old pro who would often claim that he wasn't fit enough to play. 'Boss, I've done this,' he'd say, or 'I'm not feeling too well.'

But once I'd got to know him, I worked out how to handle him. 'Keith, can you play?' I'd ask him.

'Oh, I'll play,' he'd reply.

I wouldn't say another word to him and then he'd go out and play well, more often than not. You have to know how to handle different players. As I knew from my playing days, some players will play well after getting a bollocking while others will sulk. I loved trying to gee the players up and copied what I had picked up as a player. I liked managers to sit next to me before a match and tell me exactly what they wanted me to do. When my old Sheffield Wednesday manager Harry Catterick told me, 'Swanny, you're the best centre half in England,' I felt ten feet fall when I went out there.

I took Matlock into the first round proper of the FA Cup for only the second time in the history of the club. When we drew Blackburn Rovers, I met the Matlock chairman, Cliff Britland and said to him, 'Cliff, I want you to give these players as much bonus as you can for a win. You can't lose because if we win, you've got another round.' But he wouldn't do it, despite the fact that it was a full house with over 5,000 fans packed into our tiny Causeway Lane ground. There had been a lot of rain before the game, so it was a very boggy pitch. I named David Layne as the substitute and we were 4-0 down, with about two minutes to go, when I turned to him and said, 'Go on, make a name for yourself.' He wasn't best pleased. 'Do me a favour: fuck off and leave me here will you,' he said. Blackburn, who were managed by Gordon Lee, won 4-1. They went on to win the Third Division championship that season.

I had taken David Layne to the club after we played together for a Wednesday Old Boys XI against an amateur team in Sheffield called Norton Woodseats. David scored two or three goals and I phoned him up a few days later to ask him whether he would be interested in playing for Matlock. 'I just want another look at you!' I told him. He accepted my offer and agreed to play without being paid, which was brilliant. I didn't play David on a regular basis, but he was there if I needed him and he made a few appearances.

We played in the FA Trophy, which is the non-League equivalent of the FA Cup. The competition took me back to Wembley and provided me with the undoubted highlight of my managerial career. Our long journey to the Twin Towers started with a 1-0 win at Tamworth in the third qualifying round. That was followed by a 3-0 home victory over King's Lynn in the first round. We then faced Burscough, beating them 3-1 in a replay at Causeway Lane following a 1-1 draw. A replay was also required against Ilford in the following round when, after being held to a 1-1 draw at home, we sneaked a 1-0 win at their place. We won by the same scoreline away at Goole Town in the fourth round to secure a place in the semi-finals.

We were drawn against Burton Albion in a two-legged semi. Burton, who had the former Manchester United star Ian Storey-Moore in their side, were the favourites to go through to the final. They were a bigger club than Matlock and all the talk before we faced them was that Storey-Moore was set to go to Wembley. We played the first leg at Matlock, which attracted a club record crowd of 5,123. I didn't set a good example because I was sent off in the game. Burton had a big, bustling centre forward called Doug Hickton who was backing into me, so I just gave him a little dig in the ribs and the linesman saw what happened. It was nothing really, but Hickton made a meal of it and acted as though I'd whacked him with a real good 'un. After talking to the linesman, the referee came over to me and I knew I was in trouble. 'I haven't done anything wrong, it was more or less a shove,' I protested. He wasn't listening though and showed me the red card. Burton won 1-0 and, with the return leg at their place, they must have thought they were as good as through to the final.

I was allowed to play in the return leg and Hickton, who'd play-acted to get me sent off, was frightened to death. He thought I was really going to get him this time, so he stayed away from me and didn't get a kick. It was the easiest semi-final I ever played in. Storey-Moore didn't make the impact that everyone expected because he was marked out of the game. The full-back who was on Storey-Moore couldn't wait to play against him and he kept him quiet in both legs. Peter Scott and Nick Fenoughty scored to give us a 2-0 win on the night and make it 2-1 on aggregate. We had done it, tiny Matlock were heading to Wembley!

To get to Wembley was unbelievable for a club like Matlock. The people of Matlock were going mad, putting out flags and banners. We were second from bottom when we played Scarborough at Wembley, but that was because of a fixture backlog which had left us nine or ten games behind the rest of the teams. If we won the games in hand, we'd be near the top. Scarborough looked at our League position and were very confident of beating us. I appeared on Yorkshire TV with the Scarborough chairman Don Robinson on the day before the final. 'What do you think your chances are tomorrow, Peter?' I was asked.

'If we play the way I know how we can play, there will be no problems,' I replied. 'But it's the team who gets it right on the day.'

Robinson was asked the same question. 'Oh yes, no problem, we'll win,' he confidently predicted. He was mentioning the League positions of the two teams and things like that. I had to laugh.

I decided to take all the players to Wembley on the Friday. 'We'll go and have a look at it and then you know you've been on the Wembley pitch before we go out of the dressing room, so it's not a new thing,' I told them. We had a full morning on the pitch, just walking about and taking in the scenery. It paid dividends because there were no nerves on the day of the match.

We stayed overnight, which was unheard of for Matlock, at the Carnarvon Hotel in Ealing, But I reasoned that the club was earning a lot of money, so they could afford it. We also had club blazers and slacks, as I felt it was important that the players looked smart. I wanted to keep the players relaxed, so I had a few tricks up my sleeve. In the hotel lobby on the morning of the match, I tied a fiver to a length of cotton and put it on the floor. We then sat and waited for people to spot it. It's amazing how many people looked round to check if anyone had seen them before bending down to try and pick it up. I'd then whip it away before they could get their hands on it. But one chap caught me out though when he put his foot on the note, snapped the cotton and made off with the fiver!

When we were in the dressing room at Wembley, I sat the players down and gave them a pre-match pep-talk. 'Right, I've got something else to tell you,' I said. 'You're playing at Matlock, forget Wembley. If it wants a long ball, you'll play a long 'un. We'll play exactly the way we play at Matlock.' And that's what we did.

The Scarborough side included their player-manager Ken Houghton, who was a vastly experienced League player, most notably with Hull City. Nick Barmby's father Jeff was also in their team. Scarborough were playing all the pretty stuff because they were playing at Wembley. But we played our own game and it couldn't have been better. I felt we were always in control.

Playing at Wembley for the first time in thirteen years brought a lot of memories back for me, especially going down the tunnel. The place hadn't changed; it was just how I remembered it. Every time I'd played at Wembley for England it was in front of 100,000 fans. It was a bit of a letdown that there were only 20,000 people there this time and they were all in one part of the stadium, so it was like a drop in the ocean.

Scarborough went close on a couple of occasions before Colin Oxley gave us the lead with a shot which went through the keeper's legs. We held on to our 1-0 advantage going into the interval. We had a let-off early in the second half when Scarborough's John Woodall shot wide from five yards out. As Scarborough threatened to score an equaliser, Colin Dawson made it 2-0 in the sixty-sixth minute. Mick Fenoughty's corner was headed on by Peter Scott and Dawson applied the finish. Tom Fenoughty struck a superb free-kick from about thirty-five yards to increase our lead. Tom's brother Nick rounded off the scoring with a header from an Oxley cross to complete a resounding 4-0 victory. 'Easy, easy,' chanted the Matlock supporters.

After the Scarborough chairman Don Robinson had predicted a comfortable victory for his team on the eve of the match, it was very satisfying when we went on to hammer them. We had no end of champagne in the dressing room, including some sent from Robinson, which was a nice gesture. I have to say that Scarborough were very sporting in defeat. Ken Houghton said we deserved the victory and the Scarborough supporters cheered us as we went on a lap of honour. I tried to get a bonus for the players, but the committee wouldn't have it.

To mark our Wembley triumph, we were given a civic reception, which was an unforgettable experience. We toured the streets of Matlock and adjoining villages in an open-top bus. Matlock itself was packed solid with people turning out to cheer us. Supporters lined the streets and it was a sea of blue and white in the warm spring sunshine. The Matlock Band played 'Congratulations' as we approached the county council offices. We were introduced to the various councillors and officials before walking onto the main terrace. 'We want Swanny,' the fans chanted from the grounds below the terrace, before I stepped up to the microphone. I composed myself before saying, 'When I saw Tom Fenoughty go up to receive the cup I thought, "This is Matlock Town's finest hour." I was really proud of our players. The response from everyone at Matlock during the past year – the team, the committee, the supporters – has made me proud, too. I have only been at Matlock one season, but I feel that I have been here all my life.'

In a memorable season, we also beat Glossop to win the Derbyshire Senior Cup for the first time in the club's history. I desperately wanted to get a job in the Football League and thought the triumph at Wembley would be the springboard for me to achieve that aim. I can remember being with one of my brothers, who came to watch us at Wembley, and saying, 'I can't see me not getting a League manager's job now.' I felt I was equipped to make the move up the managerial ladder and made no secret of my ambitions. As we celebrated our Wembley success, I told journalists, 'Now I believe I'm ready to be a Football League manager. But if there's no opening here, I'm ready to take a job on the Continent.' I began to apply for jobs with League clubs, but without any success.

Everyone at the club was on a high following the FA Trophy success and we entered the 1975/76 season with high hopes of doing well in the Northern Premier League.

We finished fourth that season, which was a big improvement on the previous few terms. But even though we had continued to make progress at Matlock in my second season at the club, I was still getting nowhere in my bid to break into League management. I put in for the Chesterfield manager's job when it came up. There was an old director at Chesterfield called Mr Shentall who was a friend of Matlock chairman Cliff Britland and he'd obviously tipped him off. One Saturday afternoon, before a game, Cliff came into the dressing room to have a word with me. 'I hear you've put in for the Chesterfield job,' he said. After I confirmed that I had, he said, 'Well, you've got it.' I hurried off home after the game and told my family I was going to be the new manager of Chesterfield. I waited to hear from them, but the call never came. I asked Cliff if he could shed any light on the situation. 'I can only tell you what they've told me,' he said. I eventually read that they had appointed someone, ending any hopes I had of landing the job. I applied to all lower division clubs, but the only reply I received was from Stockport. I thought to myself, 'What I've got to do is to go to another club, try and do the same as I've done with Matlock, and it might make Football League clubs sit up and take notice.' So I handed in my resignation a year after that unforgettable day at Wembley.

I went to Worksop, who were always a lower league side, taking my son Carl with me. My plan looked to be working because we finished fourth in the Northern Premier, but I then had a falling-out with the committee and walked out. We were playing Gateshead and I was asked to meet the committee before the match. At the meeting I was told to cut the wage bill by letting go of three players. I wasn't happy with the decision, but knew I couldn't do anything about it. 'Okay, I'll go away and think about it and tell you which three players are going after the game,' I said.

We played the match and afterwards I spoke to the three players I'd reluctantly decided to part with, telling them why they had to go. I told them that I didn't want them to leave, explaining that I'd been forced to reduce the wage bill. Then I got a message, telling me that the committee wanted to see me straight away in the boardroom. I went in and one of the players was stood there, so I said to the committee men, 'I'm not talking to you until this player's out of the room.' After the player was made to leave, I asked, 'Right, what's all this about then?'

'We don't think you should get rid of that player,' one of them said. 'We think you should get rid of your own son.' The suggestion made me furious.

'My own son? My own fucking son doesn't get paid. If that's how thick you are, I'm going and I don't want to come back. I'm done.'

They didn't try to stop me, so that was the end of my time at Worksop even though we were, I think, second in the Northern Premier League at the time.

The committeemen at non-League clubs were generally very good. But you'd always get one who'd try and tell you how to play the game. You'd get someone who'd come up to you before a game and say, 'I know this lad I'd like you to play, Peter.'

'Who's he play for?' I'd ask.

They'd say something like, 'The Three Horseshoes.'

When I refused to pick the player in question, the committeeman would protest and say he'd told him he could play. But I'd stand my ground and refuse to back down, however much they argued. 'Well, you can tell him he can't play, until I've seen him,' I'd say. They'd get really upset about it, but that's committeemen for you. Half of them have no idea about the game, but they think they have.

After quitting Worksop, I then went to Buxton, again taking my lad Carl with me. Before one game on a freezing cold day at Buxton, Carl couldn't tie his laces or even hold his cup of tea, so the physiotherapist rubbed his legs with whisky to warm him up. He also gave him a shot of whisky and it did the trick.

Buxton proved to be a dead-end job. They had no money and I had to get players out of the local leagues. We were getting some good players, but you've got to spend time with them to develop them and get them ready for the Northern Premier League. It just wasn't happening at Buxton, so I left.

Towards the end of 1980, I returned to Matlock for a second spell. I was asked to get rid of all the old players in order to cut the wage bill. The players were mainly ones I'd taken there during my first spell at the club and they were obviously getting old and past it. It was a hard job for me to get rid of the players I'd had success with previously, but I carried out the instructions of the committee. I had no money to replace the players I was losing, so I was getting young players from the local leagues and pubs. I had a couple of older players who were looking after the lads on the pitch and organising them.

We were losing games, but we were playing some good football and there were signs of improvement. You could see that things were on the right track. But some members of the committee came to the pub I was running in Chesterfield and told me they had decided a change of management was required. 'We want you to resign,' they said. I'd only been back there about half a season and wasn't ready to pack in. I said, 'You want me to resign? I'm building a side, why do you want me to resign?' They said that they weren't happy with the job I was doing. 'No, I'm not resigning, if you want to sack me, then sack me, but I'm not resigning.' So they sacked me. It was December 1981 and that proved to be the end of my managerial career.

With hindsight, leaving Matlock the first time was a mistake. Things had started so well for me at Matlock, winning at Wembley in my first season. It was just a pity that I was not given the opportunity to build on that success and prove myself in the League.

I would have loved to have had a crack at League management. But I think that I wasn't accepted at boardroom level because of the scandal. I never heard anything to back that up, it's just what I think. I'd served my time, but it appears that some people weren't prepared to forgive and forget.

15

Lies in *The Fix*

I'm never allowed to forget the fact that I was involved in the biggest scandal in the history of British sport. I often think about what happened and I'm regularly asked about the scandal.

Given the interest in the case, I suppose it was inevitable that someone would make a television drama based on the story and that's what happened in 1997 when the BBC screened *The Fix*. It featured comedy actor Steve Coogan, better known as the fictional character Alan Partridge, in his first serious acting role. He appeared alongside *Boon* actor Michael Elphick. Coogan played the part of reporter Mike Gabbert from *The People* and Elphick took on the role of another reporter who was involved in the case, Peter Campling.

The production was filmed at various locations in London, Sheffield and Liverpool. For some reason, Tony Kay alone was recruited to advise the production team. I didn't even know about *The Fix* until I was told that it was going to be shown. I wasn't contacted by the production people and neither was David Layne. If I had been approached, the first thing I would have done would have been to get in touch with David and Tony. That's the way I think it should be. I am still in fairly regular contact with David and as soon as I was approached to write this book, I got straight on the phone to him to tell him what was happening and he wished me the best of luck.

David phoned Tony when he heard that the film was going to be shown, trying to find out what was going to be shown. Apparently, Tony played it down. 'Oh, it's nothing,' he said.

'Well, they're advertising it, what's it all about?' David asked.

'It's all about me and Marina (his wife) and when I left Wednesday.'

'Doesn't it concern Swanny and I then?'

'No, you're not in it.'

'Okay, fair enough, forget it.'

David left it at that, thinking that whatever Tony could get out of it was up to him. The writer and director of the film, who was called Paul Greengrass, phoned David the night before it was shown. 'I've tried to make it funny and I think you'll like it,' he told him.

In the trailers for the film, it was claimed that the truth about the scandal was being told at last. I was interested to see how they had portrayed the story, so I made sure that I was sat at home in front of the television when it was aired. To say I was shocked at what I saw is an understatement. I could hardly take in what I was watching. It was so far away from the truth, it was unbelievable. The film made out that David and I encouraged Tony to fix a game, which was totally untrue. There was a scene which showed David's character saying, 'But we threw the game…' That never happened and I was livid after watching the film because it made real fools out of David and myself. David actually came out of it worse than me because it made it look as though he was the instigator for what happened, which wasn't true, so I felt sorry for him more than anything. It also made out that Tony was put under pressure to get involved in the bet, but that wasn't the case.

I thought that David and myself should have been approached before the filming got under way, to ask if we would provide any input. If Kay had picked the phone up, we would have gone in with him. We weren't bothered about the money. But I think there's no doubt that Tony was motivated by money to take part in the filming. I'm told he's been short of money since finishing playing and the last I heard he was working as a groundsman in London, so he won't be earning a lot of cash. I can only speculate how much he picked up for taking part in the production of *The Fix*. I've heard various figures mentioned, ranging from £6,000 to £10,000, but I don't know. He would no doubt have been under pressure to twist the story in order to make it juicier, but he should have refused on principle. I think it was shocking for him to take part in telling a story which simply wasn't true. As I've said previously, we all just felt we had nothing to lose by betting on Ipswich to win the game. We knew what we were doing and there should have been no suggestion from Kay that we threw the game because that was not the case.

In our younger days, Tony and I were very close. We both joined Wednesday straight from school and came up through the ranks together. We socialised a lot as well and I stayed at his parents house in Sheffield on many occasions as a young lad. But after Tony left Sheffield Wednesday to join Everton, I rarely saw him, apart from when we played against each other. After being released from prison, he went to live in Spain. I understand he was later arrested after selling a 'diamond' that turned out to be a fake. It's probably a good thing that I've never seen Tony, or even heard from him, since the film went out. I don't want anything to do with him. In fact, I hope I never see him because I might just lose it. I think if I ever met him again, face to face, I'd have to hit him. I'm that bitter about the way he blamed David and myself for what happened.

What makes things worse is that David put Tony up at his pub on several occasions when he was looking for somewhere to stay for a few days. He never charged him and David would even give him some cash for a night out if he was short, as he usually was. Soon after the film was shown, one of David's friends saw Kay in a Sheffield casino. The pair knew each other, so Kay went up to him and said, 'Ey up JB, how's it going?'

'If I were you, I would get my arse out of here, lively,' John replied. 'There are one or two in here who want to fucking whack you. Don't go down to Layne's either because you're going to cop for one down there as well.'

Apparently, he left Sheffield straight away and wasn't seen in the city again until he tried to patch things up with David in 2005. Someone David knows came into his pub one morning and asked him, 'Have you still got a gripe with Kay?'

'Well, I don't want to talk to him, if that's what you mean,' said David. 'After all this time, he's left it a bit too late.'

'I've got him in the car outside and he wants to come in for a drink. Don't you want to see him?'

'No, I'm not bothered.'

David looked out of the window and saw Kay sat there in the passenger seat. That was the first time Kay had tried to make contact with either of us since *The Fix* came out, some eight years earlier. David maintains that if Kay had come along straight after the film was shown and apologised, saying that he had made a mistake, things would have been different.

David and I tried our best to take legal action over how the story had been portrayed. Sheffield-based journalist Peter Cooper, who worked for the *Daily Mirror*, helped us.

We knew and trusted Peter from our playing days because he had travelled to matches with us regularly on the team coach. He was the type of journalist you could discuss things with and know that he wouldn't print what you had said. On our behalf, Peter explored the possibility of trying to take legal action against the film makers. They argued that as it was a drama, it didn't have to be factual and they were within their rights to do what they did.

We were clinging to the hope that a precedent had been set when the ancestors of someone wrongly portrayed in the film *Titanic* received a compensation pay-out. In the film, the ship's purser was shown shooting one of the passengers. But members of the purser's family successfully argued that he had not shot anyone. In reality, amid panic among the passengers as the ship was sinking, he fired a shot above their heads in a bid to try and restore order. Our attempts to take similar action never got off the ground and we were forced to accept there was nothing we could do about the lies told in *The Fix*.

David and I got a chance to set the record straight a few years ago when we were interviewed together for a television programme on Channel Five. The producers told us they wanted us to give our side of the story. We were desperate to have our say after seeing how the story had been falsely portrayed before and agreed to co-operate straight away. But it was disappointing because things didn't work out as we had been told. We were taken to a location in Sheffield to be interviewed and then told by one of the production people that the interview would not be shown. She explained that it was a pilot which would be used to sell the idea of doing a programme. We were told that if they then received the go-ahead, terms would be agreed with us and we would be interviewed again. We were happy to go along with it on the understanding that the interview was not going to be shown on television. But a week later, it was shown on Channel Five, so they got it for virtu-ally nothing, paying us only expenses. David phoned the production girl who had spoken to us. 'You told us it was a pilot which wouldn't be shown,' he said.

'No,' she protested, 'I said we might use it if we wanted to.'

It turned out there was nothing we could do about it and we felt let down because promises made to us had not been kept.

16

Family Tragedy

I don't know what it is about the Swan family, but we only seem to be able to produce males. It is somewhat unusual that all eight of the children my parents had were boys. Similarly, Norma and myself had an all-male brood. We were blessed with five children: Carl, Gary, Peter, Craig and Lee.

When my lads were young and playing in the school teams, I'd go and watch them. More often than not, a parent of one of the other kids playing in the team would shout out something like, 'You'll never be as good as your father, Swanny.' It was said innocently, but it would hurt the lad who was on the receiving end, whether it was Carl, Gary, Peter, Craig or Lee. I couldn't understand what they got out of making comments like that, but I suppose it regularly happens to sons of footballers.

Carl played for me at Matlock and Worksop before turning professional. It wasn't easy for him following in my footsteps because he'd get the same comments ahe had in school. They'd do it to try and put him off, but I used to tell him to not let the opposition fans get him down. 'You'll always get somebody in the crowd who wants to take a piece out of you,' I'd say. People will shout out all sorts of things to get at you, if a member of your family has done something or whatever. I'd often be spurred on by the abuse when I was playing. The more the opposition fans had a go at me, calling me a 'dirty bastard' or whatever, the more determined I was to get the ball. I don't know what fans think they're achieving when they're abusing you because it used to lift me, so it had a negative effect on their own team.

As his father, I obviously wanted to push Carl forward. I could see things in his game that perhaps others couldn't see because I was looking at him more than other players. He was an idle player and I always used to get onto him about that. Carl was the laziest footballer in training that I've ever seen. He simply wouldn't train, preferring to go out at night and play the field. He altered his ways after moving into the professional game when he joined Doncaster Rovers from Burton Albion for a nominal fee. They make them train hard in the professional game and Carl had to knuckle down and do as he was told. Billy Bremner was the manager of Doncaster at that time and he phoned to tell me he was going to sign Carl. He wanted my advice, saying, 'Is he ready to go into the first team? Give me your honest opinion.'

'Billy, what am I going to say about my own son?', I said. 'Naturally, I could just tell you to play him, to give him a push. But I'll not tell you any lies. I'll give you my honest opinion of him and say that he'll do a good job for you. Nobody will beat him in the air and yes, I think he is ready.'

Billy took my word and put Carl straight into the first team. He settled in comfortably and Billy was satisfied with his progress. Billy and I would occasionally chat on the phone and in one of our conversations he compared Carl's aerial strength to that of the legendary former Leeds and

Wales star John Charles, which was some accolade. 'I always rated John as the finest header of the ball in the game and I rate Carl in a similar mould,' he said.

At six feet three inches tall, Carl was a dominant figure in the air, but he was also confident with the ball at his feet, so he had plenty going for him. He looked set for a decent career, but he was unlucky to break his leg in training and that was the start of his fitness problems. It was a Doncaster coach who broke his leg, going over the top in a challenge for the ball. After recovering from the broken leg, Carl went out on loan to Rochdale, but he was never really the same player again. Injury problems took their toll and he was forced to retire at the age of twenty-five due to a back problem. If it hadn't been for the injuries, I think he would have progressed and Doncaster would have made a lot of money on him. That's my opinion, but as his father I may be a little biased.

Carl's now the boss of a school for the mentally handicapped. I got him into that line of work after training a mentally handicapped football team. I was asked if I would train the team for a national tournament and I agreed to do it. All they wanted me to do was to get them fit. I didn't train them at football, I just worked on their fitness. They would run and run and it was a job to stop them running! It was unbelievable. I was doing two mornings a week with them, taking them through a training routine. At that particular time, Carl was without a job after the firm he joined from school went bust, so I got him linked up with the school I was helping out. He helped me train the lads which led to a job in that field of work and he's worked his way up the ladder. He and his wife are now in charge of a special school in Scotland.

Another of my lads, Peter, was desperate to become a professional footballer. He trained hard in the hope of achieving his ambition, but I could see he hadn't got the ability to succeed. It was a great shame because all he wanted to do was become a footballer. I used to think to myself, 'How do I tell him?' I thought the only way I could do it was to prove to him that he wasn't cut out for life in professional football. I was at Matlock Town at the time and he was training with the team. He got his chance in the side when we were short of players, making his debut against Oswestry. We then played Gateshead and I decided to give him another go in the side, following some late withdrawals. Peter struggled in the game and was given a real run around. The experience made him realise that he wasn't going to make it in the game. 'I now know what you mean,' he told me afterwards. Peter now works in the building trade and Craig works as a financial adviser for an estate agent in Chesterfield.

Our youngest lad Lee was diagnosed with muscular dystrophy when he was about eighteen. It is a condition which affects the muscles because they stop developing. The stark reality of the situation is that he could die at any time. That is because the heart muscle can stop working. When he was first diagnosed, they gave him about ten years before he would be in a wheelchair. But he's still walking over twenty years later, albeit with a severe limp. He has regular checks on his condition, but the sad thing is that he is getting worse all the time. Lee gets on with life though and doesn't let it get him down. He does a lot of fishing and takes part in everything else he can do. Lee has known the situation since day one, but he never grumbles. You can see when he is in pain, but he never lets on. All of my other lads were interested in football and played the game, but Lee was never really that keen. It annoyed him when a PE teacher had a go at him in games lessons, saying, 'Come on Swanny, you'll never be as good as your father.' Whether he resented the game because of that, I don't know. As a kid, Lee was nicknamed 'Fats' because he was plump, so

I started getting him to train with me. We were running and doing weights, but that soon had to stop when I was told that it would do him more harm than good because of his condition.

Another son, Gary, went to catering college and became a chef. I had him when we first put food on at The Three Horseshoes pub in Chesterfield. He handled the catering side while I looked after the beer and it worked well. Gary was well-liked with a good sense of humour and was a natural at running a pub. He enjoyed pub life after being brought up in the ones we ran and was a brilliant barman. I would go so far as to say there was only one better than him that I've seen in my time. With a barman like Gary, you could have a pub full of people and only need one working behind the bar because he was that quick and organised. Gary also did the odd bit of labouring, working for a scrap firm and on the roads, doing pipe-laying. He was a grafter and was known as 'The Human JCB' because he could dig a hole so quickly. Gary was a big, fit lad who played football and other sports and was a good player in the local leagues. I don't think he would have made it at a higher level, but he shone in the pub teams he played in. He was a bit of a lad who could look after himself. He wouldn't look for trouble, but he could handle himself if others had a go.

As a family, we were devastated when Gary was diagnosed with cancer while still in his thirties. A tumour was found in his stomach and it turned out to be cancerous. He was given the all clear, but the cancer then spread to his lungs. He visited the doctor quite regularly and I'd take him up there. Gary knew for a long time before we did that his condition was terminal, but he never told us. If the doctor was going to say something to him, he wouldn't let me stop with him. He'd always ask me to go out of the room. I knew something was wrong, of course, but he wouldn't let me hear what the doctor had to say. The doctor obviously had to respect Gary's wishes, but he told me after he had died that he had given him so long to live.

Despite Gary's best attempts to protect us, we knew his condition was terminal. I can't tell you how hard it hits you to learn that one of your children is going to die. He lived on the coast at Chapel St Leonards with his partner, but we got him to come to our home so Norma could look after him. You feel helpless in a situation like that because you obviously try and help them as much as you can, but there's nothing you can do about the problem. We were just watching him waste away. You could see him gradually going, which was so hard to witness. But I was determined not to let Gary see how much it was affecting me. Nurses from the Macmillan organisation visited Gary during his final days. They would come every day and do what they could to ease his suffering. They did a brilliant job and I'm full of admiration for them.

Gary was thirty-nine when he died in 1998. You don't ever fully get over the loss of a loved one at such a young age, but time heals your pain that little bit. I can't help feeling bitter about losing Gary. The worst part about it is that there are some bastards alive who don't deserve to be. How can there be a God when that happens? When there are little kids in hospital, in pain and dying, it does make you wonder if there is anybody up there. He's supposed to be a God of love – why he is letting someone die young or letting a young baby suffer? It tests your faith in Christianity. I was brought up as a Christian and we'd go to church as kids, reading the bible at school. But I don't know what to think now. I'll see somebody who's a genuine person really struggling and then I'll see some bastard who might have robbed someone or committed another crime and he's leading a life of luxury. I often say to myself, 'There can't be anybody up there.'

Something unusual happened following Gary's death,
when I was offered a picture by a woman who came to
my pub. 'I've got a picture at home and I'm frightened
because there's a face in it,' she said. I told her I'd be interested in taking it off her, so she brought it in to the pub.
It's a large picture of a woodland scene and I decided to
hang it up over the fireplace. I was looking for a face and
sure enough I saw a little old woman in one corner of
the picture. But then, over the following weeks, the little
old woman disappeared and a large face emerged. It was
then that I could clearly make out the image of Gary. I
had not had the picture up very long when one of Gary's
ex-girlfriends came in to the pub. She was a girl he knew
in his schooldays and lived across from the pub. On this
particular night, she was stood at the bar and just happened
to turn and look at the picture. She broke down in tears
and ran out of the pub. I hadn't told her anything about
the picture, but she saw the image of Gary in it. Whether
someone else had told her to come in and have a look at
it, I don't know. It's there all the time when I look at the
picture. I have thought about getting a priest to have a look
at it and give me his opinion. There are times when I do
draw comfort from being able to see Gary's face. I sit with
him last thing at night, having my last drink before going
to bed, and I can see him.

My wife can't see the image and others are also sceptical.
'Well, it's what you want to see,' they'll say. The woman who
brought the picture to me said it was evil, but I don't know
really know what to think about it. Sometimes, when I'm
on my own, looking at the picture, I'll feel really cold when
I go near it and my hair stands up on end. I can't understand
why. I'll look at the picture and say, 'I'm not scared of you
Gary, why have I got to feel like this?'

Being a spiritualist, my mum would have loved it and
she'd have no doubt told me what it was all about. I'm sure

she would have had an answer to it. We used to laugh at the things she said about spiritualist matters when we were kids, but it made me think differently when she warned me that I was going to be in trouble and it turned out to be true. That made me think there must be something in it.

17

Battling with Alzheimer's

I have been diagnosed as being in the first stages of Alzheimer's. I can go way back and remember incidents from my childhood, as I've done in the writing of this book, but my short-term memory is poor. For years I would go for something upstairs and then forget about what I'd gone for. I read an article about the condition which explained that the problem usually starts that way. I decided to make an appointment to see my doctor and after undergoing a series of tests, my suspicions that I had Alzheimer's were confirmed when the diagnosis was made.

I'm on medication for the problem, which appears to have improved the state of my health. I take one pill in the morning and another at night. I think I will be taking them for the rest of my life. Unfortunately, there are side effects. I feel nauseous after taking the medication and sometimes, after taking a tablet in the morning, I'm left with a flu-like feeling for some hours. There's been a debate over whether the drugs should be readily available on the NHS. I think they should be because that's what you pay your demands and dues for when you're working. You've paid your money, so I don't think you should start having to pay for medication. It annoys me that someone who's worked all his life, saved his money and got a bank book has to pay out, but then another person, who's thrown all his money away and doesn't give a damn, gets his medication for free. It doesn't seem fair to me because it doesn't encourage people to save.

Alzheimer's is believed by some to be hereditary and my father suffered from it in his later years. It was terrible to see how it affected him, knowing there was nothing you could do about it. My mum and dad retired to Mablethorpe. She worked at a café round the corner from the house they bought. We used to go over and visit them quite regularly. When my dad had an Alzheimer's problem in his early eighties, Norma and I looked after him. It affects your sleeping when you have Alzheimer's, so he would wander around at night when he couldn't get to sleep. We would then take it in turns to keep an eye on him, to make sure he was okay. One night it would be my turn to get out of bed and see to him and the following night, Norma would take over the responsibility. When neither of us heard him get up in the night, he would start striking matches to help him see where he was going, instead of putting the light switch on. Then he started to light paper to use as a torch. It was frightening because he could have set fire to the building, but he couldn't remember what he had done. We were both working in the pub and we weren't getting much sleep. Because of that and the fact that none of the rest of the family were able to look after him, I had to have my dad put in a care home. But all he did was sleep there because I brought him out every day. He lived until he was eighty-six.

While some people insist Alzheimer's is a hereditary problem, others have suggested that my career as a foot-baller could be to blame. When the old West Brom and England centre forward Jeff Astle died a few years ago, it was claimed that heading the ball regularly had caused a brain tumour. I think that is feasible because heading was a big part of his game and balls were heavy in those days. If you didn't head the ball on the right spot, it was a hell of a knock, especially if it was wet. Who knows, heading a heavy leather ball many times in my career might be the cause of my Alzheimer's problem.

One of the repercussions of having Alzheimer's is that I've had to surrender my driving licence. I'm capable of driving, but something might happen which results in an accident. It's very frustrating to lose your independence, but I accept that it's not worth taking the risk. The danger of driving in my condition was brought home to me following an incident when I couldn't find my car. I parked up in Chesterfield town centre for a short period and then planned to return to my car, only to realise that I had absolutely no idea where I'd parked. I must have walked the streets for a couple of hours, searching all over the place for my car, before giving up. I then had to take a taxi back to my pub a few miles away and got one of my lads to drive me back into the town centre where we eventually located the missing vehicle.

The condition is so frustrating because things can go totally blank. I can talk to someone and arrange to meet them a few hours later, only to forget about the plans within minutes. A couple of friends, who I hadn't seen for a long time, called in to see me one day. They delivered the sad news that a mutual friend had died and they wanted to arrange for some food to be laid on at my pub after the funeral. As they were going out of the door, I'd forgotten everything they'd said to me. 'When you see Dave, tell him I'm going to smack him,' I said to them as they went out of the door. They just laughed and it was only when I went back upstairs that it dawned on me what had happened. 'I've just said something terrible,' I told Norma. 'I've joked that I'm going to smack Dave and it's him who's died.' I had forgotten straight away, which is what happens. My long-term memory is fine because I can remember a hell of a lot from when I was a kid. But I can put something down and then forget where it is.

Alzheimer's cases appear to be on the increase in today's society, affecting around 400,000 people in the UK. The problem was highlighted in a *Coronation Street* storyline when the 'Mike Baldwin' character had the condition. He was shown losing his short-term memory and with his health deteriorating until he died. Some of the lads in my pub picked up on this and would call me 'Baldwin'. 'How are you Mike?' they would say, the twats! My Alzheimer's problem is only slight, but people do get like Mike Baldwin and that's what might happen to me in future years.

I was approached by someone who asked me whether I would be prepared to be interviewed for a television programme they were doing on Alzheimer's. I told them that I would gladly take part, without a fee, in order to let people know more about the condition and how if affects people. But I'm still waiting to hear whether they are going ahead with it.

There's always something happening with your health, especially when you get older. As well as my problem with Alzheimer's, I also take a tablet for my prostate. There's a history of prostate problems in my family. I was given the option of having an operation or taking the tablets. My brothers and my father had operations, but I don't want to have surgery. I've been told that if I keep taking the tablets, I won't need an operation. Despite my health worries and the fact that I'm seventy next birthday, I still feel young. When I was a kid, a fifty-year-old man was old. My grandmother, when she was fifty or sixty, seemed a very old person. But it's not like that any more. I could still go jogging now if I wanted to. I do a lot of walking, taking the dog out along the canal next to our pub. I don't like sitting about because you can soon get in a rut where you just sit there and watch television or whatever, which is no good for you.

I amassed a collection of memorabilia from my time in the game and put a number of items on display inside a cabinet in my pub lounge. Customers used to like looking at the various shirts, caps and medals and it was a good talking point. But I then decided to sell most of the collection after talking to members of my family. I reasoned that there was no way of splitting the collection fairly and I wanted to avoid the possibility of arguments within the family. It wasn't an easy decision by any means, but I couldn't think of a fair way of dividing the collection. My lad Peter suggested a lucky dip, putting numbers in a bag, with whoever picking out the right number getting the lot. But I didn't like that idea because I felt it could have led to some resentment. After much discussion, various items were put up for auction at Christie's. I decided to auction my Second Division Championship winner's medal and three Inter-League medals, along with shirts I had swapped with three legendary players: Pelé, Eusebio and John Charles. The items were sent to Christie's in a parcel and they went under the hammer at an auction of sports memorabilia in September 2002. I didn't attend the auction, but one of my lads went. The items auctioned on my behalf raised a four-figure sum. I thought it might have been more, to be honest. People at that time were talking about the sort of money football memorabilia was fetching, so I was a bit disappointed with the outcome. I was surprised that John Charles' shirt, from an Inter-League match when he was playing in Italy, fetched more than Pelé's.

I kept a few items back for my lads and they've each got an England cap. I also kept an England shirt. Unfortunately, after giving my England blazer to a member of my family, it disappeared when he died. It was a dark blazer which featured the Three Lions in a gold-coloured thread on one of the breast pockets. I wrote to the FA, explaining what had happened and asking if I could buy an England badge to put on my blazer. I didn't receive a reply, so I wrote another letter. But again, I heard nothing. I phoned Lancaster Gate and asked the message to be passed on to the relevant person, but I still received no response to my request. I was disappointed with the FA's attitude over the matter. I would have thought that I'd have at least had the courtesy of a reply after playing 19 times for England. I'd love a badge to put on my blazer, but I'm resigned to the fact that I won't be able to obtain one now. Whether the bribery case had anything to do with the lack of co-operation from the FA, I don't know.

Another item of clothing from my England days which went missing was a white tracksuit. When I went for training with the England squad, they wouldn't let you take the kit away with you. It had to be left there. The only item you were able to take home was the tracksuit, which was made of a thick, fleecy material. It wasn't for training in; it was supposed to be worn after training to keep you warm. It was a brilliant tracksuit, but unfortunately mine was pinched.

People often say to me, 'Don't you get fed up with people coming up to you all the time and talking about football?' The answer is that I'll talk all day to those who want to listen to what I have to say. I only get fed up with the ones who think they know it all. They tend to want to try and test you and pull you down a little bit.

I think today's game on the whole is a much better standard than when I played. There are some skilful players around today and I would say they are generally more skilful than in my day. There were skilful players when I played of course, but not like they are today. I like the present-day game, but I just wish they wouldn't cheat. If it wasn't for the cheats in the game, with all the diving that goes on, it would be 100 per cent. I think referees could cut it out because they've only got to keep sending off the players who offend. With the use of television cameras they have now, incidents can be viewed from all angles. You didn't really get much diving in our day. The only player I can remember who had a reputation for diving was a Fulham winger called Graham Leggatt. We were always warned about him before the game when we played Fulham because he regularly went down in the area and won a penalty. You didn't even have to touch Leggatt for him to go down. In a crowded area, if you went near him, he would go over as if he'd been pole-axed. After winning the penalty, he would then get up laughing. In fairness to the referees, it was difficult for them to see what had happened in a crowded area.

I hate to see players go down when they haven't been touched. A lot of it, in my opinion, has come into the English game since the arrival of foreign players. When you were playing against foreign opposition in my day, you only had to go near the player and he would go down to try and win a free-kick or a penalty. When all the foreign players started coming over to England, I thought it had a positive effect initially because we learned a lot from them. But I think there are now too many foreigners in the English game because they are limiting the opportunities for home-grown players. There aren't as many coming through as there used to be.

When England play, I like to watch John Terry because he reads the game well and is the old-fashioned type of hard centre half. I think he would have fancied playing in my era against the big, tough centre forwards. Rio Ferdinand is a good centre half as well, but I think he'd be a lot better with a bit more aggression. A centre half doesn't need to be dirty, but he needs to put fear into the opposition. I'm a fan of Steven Gerrard because he's a brilliant player who leads by example. He also seems like a straightforward lad who hasn't got above himself, so I'd like to meet him.

I'm glad that the FA went for an English coach in Steve McClaren following Sven-Goran Eriksson's departure. I could never understand why a foreigner was appointed. It just didn't seem right to me. I believe the England coach should always been an Englishman.

I've been back to Sheffield Wednesday a few times and have always been treated well by people at the club. But I rarely go to games now, preferring mainly to watch football on the box. I've been dismayed by Wednesday's demise in recent years as they've wrestled with mounting debts. But the situation appears to be improving under chairman Dave Allen and hopefully they can regain their place in the top flight. Wednesday are a Premier League club and I'd love to see them back where they belong.

Across the city, I'm not keen on Sheffield United manager Neil Warnock who used to come into my pub. Warnock insulted me at a dinner in honour of legendary Sheffield United defender Joe Shaw. Having greatly admired Joe in his playing days, I decided to take a table at the dinner and arranged to take a number of regulars from my pub. When Warnock stood up to give a speech, he commented that Joe 'didn't need to hitch up his shorts to stand out'. I felt insulted by that and felt that I couldn't stay a moment longer in Warnock's presence. Otherwise, I would have had to hit him because I was so angry.

I went over to Joe to apologise for having to make an early exit and wished him well. Warnock deserves credit for what he has achieved in management, but I don't like him as a person and from what I understand, there are not many people in the game who have much time for him.

I still worked behind the bar of my pub, The Mill, in Brimington, Chesterfield, until quite recently. But I've now handed over the running of the pub to my son Peter, who is making a go of it. Norma and I still live at the pub, but with no day-to-day responsibilities, we're able to go and see friends and family more often in our retirement.

Epilogue

Everybody makes mistakes and I made a mistake I'll never forget. It's one I've had to live with. I knew it was against the rules to bet on a game I was involved in, so I don't blame anybody, only myself.

Why was I tempted to make some money from gambling? Well, it's a short career as a footballer and you don't know what's going to happen. One minute you're at the top of the world and then you could suffer an injury in training and see your career come to an end. I looked upon the bet as easy money, never thinking for one moment that it would prove to be my undoing. David Layne and Tony Kay will tell you the same. It was a damn silly thing to do, but we paid a heavy price because they wanted to make an example of us. I'm still bitter over how we were penalised. Instead of just one punishment, we got three. We were sent to prison, fined and banned from playing.

We didn't take a bribe, but all three of us were found guilty of bribery, which still rankles. I feel very bitter towards *The People* and Jimmy Gauld because they ruined my life. To this day, if I ever met Gauld, I'd probably get myself in trouble. I think I'd make a mess of him, even now. David

Layne tried to contact him to get some information he wanted, but he wouldn't speak to him.

With the money players earn today, it's highly unlikely they would be tempted to risk everything for a bet. But those who aren't among the high earners could be tempted. The chance to earn big money is a temptation for anybody, so you never know.

Playing football for a living is a brilliant career, especially if you're playing in the top flight and doing well. Football gave me a chance to experience things I could never have dreamed of when I was growing up as a kid in a South Yorkshire mining village. We were treated like film stars, staying in the best hotels and being taken to shows. That set you apart from your working class background. If I hadn't made it in the game, I'd have probably remained in my job as a miner in the village where I was brought up. Being a footballer helped me climb the ladder and opened up a new world for me, allowing me to visit places and experience things I would have otherwise missed out on. I might have never even gone abroad if it had not been for football. I'd love to go back to the years when I was a footballer because there's nothing better than running out in front of a big crowd and soaking up the atmosphere. It was brilliant and, given the chance, I'd do it all again.

I know I will always be associated with the scandal, but I hope that people will also remember me for my footballing ability. I achieved my childhood ambition of becoming a professional footballer, played for a top club and represented my country 19 times. Nobody can ever take that away from me.

Writing this book has given me the chance to relive some wonderful moments from my career. There have been many lies told about the scandal, so I wanted to put that right. As I'm now in my seventieth year, it seemed the right time to tell my story. I'm pleased to have been given the opportunity to set the record straight.

Career Statistics

	LEAGUE		FA CUP		LEAGUE CUP		FAIRS CUP	
	APPS	GOALS	APPS	GOALS	APPS	GOALS	APPS	GOALS
SHEFFIELD WEDNESDAY								
1955/56	4	0	0	0	No competition		No competition	
1956/57	5	0	0	0	No competition		No competition	
1957/58	13	0	1	0	No competition		No competition	
1958/59	39	0	0	0	No competition		No competition	
1959/60	42	0	5	0	No competition		No competition	
1960/61	36	0	0	0	No competition		No competition	
1961/62	40	0	4	0	No competition		6	0
1962/63	42	0	3	0	No competition		No competition	
1963/64	39	0	1	0	No competition		4	0
1972/73	13+2 sub	0	0	0	2	0	No competition	
Total:	275	0	14	0	2	0	10	0
BURY								
1973/74	35	2	0	0	4	0	No competition	
Career Total:	310	2	14	0	6	0	10	0

FOOTBALL LEAGUE SIDE

6 appearances:

DATE	OPPOSITION
4 November 1959	League of Ireland
1 November 1960	Italian League
22 March 1961	Scottish League
11 October 1961	League of Ireland
8 November 1961	Italian League
21 March 1962	Scottish League

ENGLAND RECORD

1 Youth cap:

DATE	OPPOSITION
21 November 1954	Holland

3 Under-23 caps:

DATE	OPPOSITION
11 November 1959	France
2 March 1960	Scotland
16 March 1960	Holland

Career Statistics

19 full caps:

Date	Opposition	Competition	Result	Venue
11 May 1960	Yugoslavia	Friendly	3-3	Wembley
15 May 1960	Spain	Friendly	0-3	Madrid
22 May 1960	Hungary	Friendly	0-2	Budapest
8 October 1960	Northern Ireland	Home Championship	5-2	Belfast
19 October 1960	Luxembourg	World Cup Qualifier	9-0	Luxembourg
26 October 1960	Spain	Friendly	4-2	Wembley
23 November 1960	Wales	Home Championship	5-1	Wembley
15 April 1961	Scotland	Home Championship	9-3	Wembley
10 May 1961	Mexico	Friendly	8-0	Wembley
21 May 1961	Portugal	World Cup Qualifier	1-1	Lisbon
24 May 1961	Italy	Friendly	3-2	Rome
27 May 1961	Austria	Friendly	1-3	Vienna
28 September 1961	Luxembourg	World Cup Qualifier	4-1	Highbury
14 October 1961	Wales	Home Championship	1-1	Cardiff
25 October 1961	Portugal	World Cup Qualifier	2-0	Wembley
22 November 1961	Northern Ireland	Home Championship	1-1	Wembley
4 April 1962	Austria	Friendly	3-1	Wembley
14 April 1962	Scotland	Home Championship	0-2	Glasgow
9 May 1962	Switzerland	Friendly	3-1	Wembley

Other titles published by Stadia

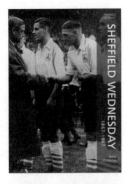

Sheffield Wednesday 1897-1967
NICK JOHNSON

This collection charts the first 100 years of Sheffield Wednesday FC, from its birth as an offshoot of a cricket club through to Football League and FA Cup triumphs, featuring insights into the everyday life of the players and the club. Included in the collection are team groups, action shots, player portraits and photographs of the Hillsborough stadium as it has been developed, with supporting text by Sheffield-born journalist Nick Johnson.

0 7524 2720 2

Voices of '66 Memories of England's World Cup
NORMAN SHIEL

Still remembered as England's finest hour, the summer of 1966 remains for many a very special moment in their lives. By recording the recollections of people who were involved with and affected by England's World Cup, this book captures the heady days when football actually came home. Including reminiscences from fans, players, administrators and television commentator Kenneth Wolstenholme, as well as many illustrations, this book will breathe life into a vital part of England's sporting heritage.

0 7524 3929 4

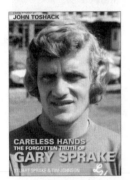

Careless Hands The Forgotten Truth of Gary Sprake
STUART SPRAKE & TIM JOHNSON

The goalkeeper of the triumphant Leeds team of the late 1960s and early '70s, Gary Sprake played in over 500 matches for the club, winning domestic and European honours, and made 37 appearances for Wales – yet many fans still remember him as 'Careless Hands', his name associated with goalkeeping gaffes and the infamous Don Revie match-fixing scandal. This authorised biography at last gives his side of the story and reminds us of the forgotten truth about this often unfairly maligned player.

0 7524 3690 2

Yorkshire County Cricket Club 100 Greats
MICK POPE & PAUL DYSON

This book features 100 of the cricketers who have shaped Yorkshire CCC. From George Anderson, who first played for Yorkshire in 1850 – before the official club was constituted – through to Matthew Hoggard, who received his county cap in 2000, there have been many wonderful players, including the likes of Boycott, Trueman and Rhodes. Featuring biographies, statistics and illustrations, this is essential reading for all Tykes.

0 7524 2179 4

If you are interested in purchasing other books published by Stadia, or in case you have difficulty finding any Stadia books in your local bookshop, you can also place orders directly through the Tempus Publishing website
www.tempus-publishing.com

If you are interested in purchasing other books published by Stadia,
or in case you have difficulty finding any Stadia books in your local
bookshop, you can also place orders directly through the Tempus
Publishing website

www.tempus-publishing.com